The Speeches of President Dwight D. Eisenhower

Contents

Chapter 1

Inaugural Addresses

1.1 Dwight Eisenhower's First Inaugural Address

My friends, before I begin the expression of those thoughts that I deem appropriate to this moment, would you permit me the privilege of uttering a little private prayer of my own. And I ask that you bow your heads:

Almighty God, as we stand here at this moment my future associates in the executive branch of government join me in beseeching that Thou will make full and complete our dedication to the service of the people in this throng, and their fellow citizens everywhere.

Give us, we pray, the power to discern clearly right from wrong, and allow all our words and actions to be governed thereby, and by the laws of this land. Especially we pray that our concern shall be for all the people regardless of station, race, or calling.

May cooperation be permitted and be the mutual aim of those who, under the concepts of our Constitution, hold to differing political faiths; so that all may work for the good of our beloved country and Thy glory. Amen.

My fellow citizens:

The world and we have passed the midway point of a century of continuing challenge. We sense with all our faculties that forces of good and evil are massed and armed and opposed as rarely before in history.

This fact defines the meaning of this day. We are summoned by this honored and historic ceremony to witness more than the act of one citizen swearing his oath of service, in the presence of God. We are called as a people to give testimony in the sight of the world to our faith that the future shall belong to the free.

Since this century's beginning, a time of tempest has seemed to come upon the continents of the earth. Masses of Asia have awakened to strike off shackles of the past. Great nations of Europe have fought their bloodiest wars. Thrones have toppled and their vast empires have disappeared. New nations have been born.

For our own country, it has been a time of recurring trial. We have grown in power and in responsibility. We have passed through the anxieties of depression and of war to a summit unmatched in man's history. Seeking to secure peace in the world, we have had to fight through the forests of the Argonne, to the shores of Iwo Jima, and to the cold mountains of Korea.

In the swift rush of great events, we find ourselves groping to know the full sense and meaning of these times in which we live. In our quest of understanding, we beseech God's guidance. We summon all our knowledge of the past and we scan all signs of the future. We bring all our wit and all our will to meet the question:

How far have we come in man's long pilgrimage from darkness toward light? Are we nearing the light—a day of freedom and of peace for all mankind? Or are the shadows of another night closing in upon us?

Great as are the preoccupations absorbing us at home, concerned as we are with matters that deeply affect our livelihood today and our vision of the future, each of these domestic problems is dwarfed by, and often even created by, this question that involves all humankind.

This trial comes at a moment when man's power to achieve good or to inflict evil surpasses the brightest hopes and the sharpest fears of all ages. We can turn rivers in their courses, level mountains to the plains. Oceans and land and sky are avenues for our colossal commerce. Disease diminishes and life lengthens.

Yet the promise of this life is imperiled by the very genius that has made it possible. Nations amass wealth. Labor sweats to create—and turns out devices to level not only mountains but also cities. Science seems ready to confer upon us, as its final gift, the power to erase human life from this planet.

At such a time in history, we who are free must proclaim anew our faith. This faith is the abiding creed of our fathers. It is our faith in the deathless dignity of man, governed by eternal moral and natural laws.

This faith defines our full view of life. It establishes, beyond debate, those gifts of the Creator that are man's inalienable rights, and that make all men equal in His sight.

In the light of this equality, we know that the virtues most cherished by free people—love of truth, pride of work, devotion to country—all are treasures equally precious in the lives of the most humble and of the most exalted. The men who mine coal and fire furnaces and balance ledgers and turn lathes and pick cotton and heal the sick and plant corn—all serve as proudly, and as profitably, for America as the statesmen who draft treaties and the legislators who enact laws.

This faith rules our whole way of life. It decrees that we, the people, elect leaders not to rule but to serve. It asserts that we have the right to choice of our own work and to the reward of our own toil. It inspires the initiative that makes our productivity the wonder of the world. And it warns that any man who seeks to deny equality among all his brothers betrays the spirit of the free and invites the mockery of the tyrant.

It is because we, all of us, hold to these principles that the political changes accomplished this day do not imply turbulence, upheaval or disorder. Rather this change expresses a purpose of strengthening our dedication and devotion to the precepts of our founding documents, a conscious renewal of faith in our country and in the watchfulness of a Divine Providence.

The enemies of this faith know no god but force, no devotion but its use. They tutor men in treason. They feed upon the hunger of others. Whatever defies them, they torture, especially the truth.

Here, then, is joined no argument between slightly differing philosophies. This conflict strikes directly at the faith of our fathers and the lives of our sons. No principle or treasure that we hold, from the spiritual knowledge of our free schools and churches to the creative magic of free labor and capital, nothing lies safely beyond the reach of this struggle.

Freedom is pitted against slavery; lightness against the dark.

The faith we hold belongs not to us alone but to the free of all the world. This common bond binds the grower of rice in Burma and the planter of wheat in Iowa, the shepherd in southern Italy and the mountaineer in the Andes. It confers a common dignity upon the French soldier who dies in Indo-China, the British soldier killed in Malaya, the American life given in Korea.

We know, beyond this, that we are linked to all free peoples not merely by a noble idea but by a simple need. No free people can for long cling to any privilege or enjoy any safety in economic solitude. For all our own material might, even we need markets in the world for the surpluses of our farms and our factories. Equally, we need for these same farms and factories vital materials and products of distant lands. This basic law of interdependence, so manifest in the commerce of peace, applies with thousand-fold intensity in the event of war.

So we are persuaded by necessity and by belief that the strength of all free peoples lies in unity; their danger, in discord.

To produce this unity, to meet the challenge of our time, destiny has laid upon our country the responsibility of the free world's leadership.

So it is proper that we assure our friends once again that, in the discharge of this responsibility, we Americans know and we observe the difference between world leadership and imperialism; between firmness and truculence; between a thoughtfully calculated goal and spasmodic reaction to the stimulus of emergencies.

We wish our friends the world over to know this above all: we face the threat—not with dread and confusion—but with confidence and conviction.

We feel this moral strength because we know that we are not helpless prisoners of history. We are free men. We shall remain free, never to be proven guilty of the one capital offense against freedom, a lack of stanch faith.

In pleading our just cause before the bar of history and in pressing our labor for world peace, we shall be guided by certain fixed principles.

These principles are:

(1) Abhorring war as a chosen way to balk the purposes of those who threaten us, we hold it to be the first task of statesmanship to develop the strength that will deter the forces of aggression and promote the conditions of peace. For, as it must be the supreme purpose of all free men, so it must be the dedication of their leaders, to save humanity from preying upon itself.

In the light of this principle, we stand ready to engage with any and all others in joint effort to remove the causes of mutual fear and distrust among nations, so as to make possible drastic reduction of armaments. The sole requisites for undertaking such effort are that—in their purpose—they be aimed logically and honestly toward secure peace for all; and that—in their result— they provide methods by which every participating nation will prove good faith in carrying out its pledge.

(2) Realizing that common sense and common decency alike dictate the futility of appeasement, we shall never try to placate an aggressor by the false and wicked bargain of trading honor for security. Americans, indeed all free men, remember that in the final choice a soldier's pack is not so heavy a burden as a prisoner's chains.

(3) Knowing that only a United States that is strong and immensely productive can help defend freedom in our world, we view our Nation's strength and security as a trust upon which rests the hope of free men everywhere. It is the firm duty of each of our free citizens and of every free citizen everywhere to place the cause of his country before the comfort, the convenience of himself.

(4) Honoring the identity and the special heritage of each nation in the world, we shall never use our strength to try to impress upon another people our own cherished political and economic institutions.

(5) Assessing realistically the needs and capacities of proven friends of freedom, we shall strive to help them to achieve their own security and well-being. Likewise, we shall count upon them to assume, within the limits of their resources, their full and just burdens in the common defense of freedom.

(6) Recognizing economic health as an indispensable basis of military strength and the free world's peace, we shall strive to foster everywhere, and to practice ourselves, policies that encourage productivity and profitable trade. For the impoverishment of any single people in the world means danger to the well-being of all other peoples.

(7) Appreciating that economic need, military security and political wisdom combine to suggest regional groupings of free peoples, we hope, within the framework of the United Nations, to help strengthen such special bonds the world over. The nature of these ties must vary with the different problems of different areas.

In the Western Hemisphere, we enthusiastically join with all our neighbors in the work of perfecting a community of fraternal trust and common purpose.

In Europe, we ask that enlightened and inspired leaders of the Western nations strive with renewed vigor to make the unity of their peoples a reality. Only as free Europe unitedly marshals its strength can it effectively safeguard, even with our help, its spiritual and cultural heritage.

(8) Conceiving the defense of freedom, like freedom itself, to be one and indivisible, we hold all continents and peoples in equal regard and honor. We reject any insinuation that one race or another, one people or another, is in any sense inferior or expendable.

(9) Respecting the United Nations as the living sign of all people's hope for peace, we shall strive to make it not merely an eloquent symbol but an effective force. And in our quest for an honorable peace, we shall neither compromise, nor tire, nor ever cease.

By these rules of conduct, we hope to be known to all peoples.

By their observance, an earth of peace may become not a vision but a fact.

This hope—this supreme aspiration—must rule the way we live.

We must be ready to dare all for our country. For history does not long entrust the care of freedom to the weak or the timid. We must acquire proficiency in defense and display stamina in purpose.

We must be willing, individually and as a Nation, to accept whatever sacrifices may be required of us. A people that values its privileges above its principles soon loses both.

These basic precepts are not lofty abstractions, far removed from matters of daily living. They are laws of spiritual strength that generate and define our material strength. Patriotism means equipped forces and a prepared citizenry. Moral stamina means more energy and more productivity, on the farm and in the factory. Love of liberty means the guarding of every resource that makes freedom possible—from the sanctity of our families and the wealth of our soil to the genius of our scientists.

And so each citizen plays an indispensable role. The productivity of our heads, our hands, and our hearts is the source of all the strength we can command, for both the enrichment of our lives and the winning of the peace.

No person, no home, no community can be beyond the reach of this call. We are summoned to act in wisdom and in conscience, to work with industry, to teach with persuasion, to preach with conviction, to weigh our every deed with care and with compassion. For this truth must be clear before us: whatever America hopes to bring to pass in the world must first come to pass in the heart of America.

The peace we seek, then, is nothing less than the practice and fulfillment of our whole faith among ourselves and in our dealings with others. This signifies more than the stilling of guns, easing the sorrow of war. More than escape from death, it is a way of life. More than a haven for the weary, it is a hope for the brave.

This is the hope that beckons us onward in this century of trial. This is the work that awaits us all, to be done with bravery, with charity, and with prayer to Almighty God.

1.2 Dwight Eisenhower's Second Inaugural Address

Mr. Chairman, Mr. Vice President, Mr. Chief Justice, Mr. Speaker, members of my family and friends, my countrymen, and the friends of my country, wherever they may be, we meet again, as upon a like moment four years ago, and again you have witnessed my solemn oath of service to you.

I, too, am a witness, today testifying in your name to the principles and purposes to which we, as a people, are pledged.

Before all else, we seek, upon our common labor as a nation, the blessings of Almighty God. And the hopes in our hearts fashion the deepest prayers of our whole people.

May we pursue the right—without self-righteousness.

May we know unity—without conformity.

May we grow in strength—without pride in self.

May we, in our dealings with all peoples of the Earth, ever speak truth and serve justice.

And so shall America—in the sight of all men of good will—prove true to the honorable purposes that bind and rule us as a people in all this time of trial through which we pass.

We live in a land of plenty, but rarely has this Earth known such peril as today.

In our nation, work and wealth abound. Our population grows. Commerce crowds our rivers and rails, our skies, harbors, and highways. Our soil is fertile, our agriculture productive. The air rings with the song of our industry—rolling mills and blast furnaces, dynamos, dams, and assembly lines—the chorus of America the bountiful.

This is our home—yet this is not the whole of our world. For our world is where our full destiny lies—with men, of all people, and all nations, who are or would be free. And for them—and so for us—this is no time of ease or of rest.

In too much of the Earth there is want, discord, danger. New forces and new nations stir and strive across the Earth, with power to bring, by their fate, great good or great evil to the free world's future. From the deserts of North Africa to the islands of the South Pacific one third of all mankind has entered upon an historic struggle for a new freedom; freedom from grinding poverty. Across all continents, nearly a billion people seek, sometimes almost in desperation, for the skills and knowledge and assistance by which they may satisfy from their own resources, the material wants common to all mankind.

No nation, however old or great, escapes this tempest of change and turmoil. Some, impoverished by the recent World War, seek to restore their means of livelihood. In the heart of Europe, Germany still stands tragically divided. So is the whole continent divided. And so, too, is all the world.

The divisive force is International Communism and the power that it controls.

The designs of that power, dark in purpose, are clear in practice. It strives to seal forever the fate of those it has enslaved. It strives to break the ties that unite the free. And it strives to capture—to exploit for its own greater power—all forces of change in the world, especially the needs of the hungry and the hopes of the oppressed.

Yet the world of International Communism has itself been shaken by a fierce and mighty force: the readiness of men who love freedom to pledge their lives to that love. Through the night of their bondage, the unconquerable will of heroes has struck with the swift, sharp thrust of lightning. Budapest is no longer merely the name of a city; henceforth it is a new and shining symbol of man's yearning to be free.

Thus across all the globe there harshly blow the winds of change. And, we—though fortunate be our lot—know that we can never turn our backs to them.

We look upon this shaken Earth, and we declare our firm and fixed purpose—the building of a peace with justice in a world where moral law prevails.

The building of such a peace is a bold and solemn purpose. To proclaim it is easy. To serve it will be hard. And to attain it, we must be aware of its full meaning—and ready to pay its full price.

We know clearly what we seek, and why.

We seek peace, knowing that peace is the climate of freedom. And now, as in no other age, we seek it because we have been warned, by the power of modern weapons, that peace may be the only climate possible for human life itself.

Yet this peace we seek cannot be born of fear alone: it must be rooted in the lives of nations. There must be justice, sensed and shared by all peoples, for, without justice the world can know only a tense and unstable truce. There must be law, steadily invoked and respected by all nations, for without law, the world promises only such meager justice as the pity of the strong upon the weak. But the law of which we speak, comprehending the values of freedom, affirms the equality of all nations, great and small.

Splendid as can be the blessings of such a peace, high will be its cost: in toil patiently sustained, in help honorably given, in sacrifice calmly borne.

We are called to meet the price of this peace.

To counter the threat of those who seek to rule by force, we must pay the costs of our own needed military strength, and help to build the security of others.

We must use our skills and knowledge and, at times, our substance, to help others rise from misery, however far the scene of suffering may be from our shores. For wherever in the world a people knows desperate want, there must appear at least the spark of hope, the hope of progress—or there will surely rise at last the flames of conflict.

We recognize and accept our own deep involvement in the destiny of men everywhere. We are accordingly pledged to honor, and to strive to fortify, the authority of the United Nations. For in that body rests the best hope of our age for the assertion of that law by which all nations may live in dignity.

And, beyond this general resolve, we are called to act a responsible role in the world's great concerns or conflicts— whether they touch upon the affairs of a vast region, the fate of an island in the Pacific, or the use of a canal in the Middle East. Only in respecting the hopes and cultures of others will we practice the equality of all nations. Only as we show willingness and wisdom in giving counsel—in receiving counsel—and in sharing burdens, will we wisely perform the work of peace.

For one truth must rule all we think and all we do. No people can live to itself alone. The unity of all who dwell in freedom is their only sure defense. The economic need of all nations—in mutual dependence—makes isolation an impossibility; not even America's prosperity could long survive if other nations did not also prosper. No nation can longer be a fortress, lone and strong and safe. And any people, seeking such shelter for themselves, can now build only their own prison.

Our pledge to these principles is constant, because we believe in their rightness.

We do not fear this world of change. America is no stranger to much of its spirit. Everywhere we see the seeds of the same growth that America itself has known. The American experiment has, for generations, fired the passion and the courage of millions elsewhere seeking freedom, equality, and opportunity. And the American story of material progress has helped excite the longing of all needy peoples for some satisfaction of their human wants. These hopes that we have helped to inspire, we can help to fulfill.

In this confidence, we speak plainly to all peoples.

We cherish our friendship with all nations that are or would be free. We respect, no less, their independence. And when, in time of want or peril, they ask our help, they may honorably receive it; for we no more seek to buy their sovereignty than we would sell our own. Sovereignty is never bartered among freemen.

We honor the aspirations of those nations which, now captive, long for freedom. We seek neither their military alliance nor any artificial imitation of our society. And they can know the warmth of the welcome that awaits them when, as must be, they join again the ranks of freedom.

We honor, no less in this divided world than in a less tormented time, the people of Russia. We do not dread, rather do we welcome, their progress in education and industry. We wish them success in their demands for more intellectual freedom, greater security before their own laws, fuller enjoyment of the rewards of their own toil. For as such things come to pass, the more certain will be the coming of that day when our peoples may freely meet in friendship.

So we voice our hope and our belief that we can help to heal this divided world. Thus may the nations cease to live in trembling before the menace of force. Thus may the weight of fear and the weight of arms be taken from the burdened shoulders of mankind.

This, nothing less, is the labor to which we are called and our strength dedicated.

And so the prayer of our people carries far beyond our own frontiers, to the wide world of our duty and our destiny.

May the light of freedom, coming to all darkened lands, flame brightly—until at last the darkness is no more.

May the turbulence of our age yield to a true time of peace, when men and nations shall share a life that honors the dignity of each, the brotherhood of all.

Chapter 2

State of the Union Addresses

2.1   Dwight D. Eisenhower's First State of the Union Address

Mr. President, Mr. Speaker, Members of the Eighty-third Congress:

I welcome the honor of appearing before you to deliver my first message to the Congress.

It is manifestly the joint purpose of the congressional leadership and of this administration to justify the summons to governmental responsibility issued last November by the American people. The grand labors of this leadership will involve:

Application of America's influence in world affairs with such fortitude and such foresight that it will deter aggression and eventually secure peace;

Establishment of a national administration of such integrity and such efficiency that its honor at home will ensure respect abroad;

Encouragement of those incentives that inspire creative initiative in our economy, so that its productivity may fortify freedom everywhere; and

Dedication to the well-being of all our citizens and to the attainment of equality of opportunity for all, so that our Nation will ever act with the strength of unity in every task to which it is called.

The purpose of this message is to suggest certain lines along which our joint efforts may immediately be directed toward realization of these four ruling purposes.

The time that this administration has been in office has been too brief to permit preparation of a detailed and comprehensive program of recommended action to cover all phases of the responsibilities that devolve upon our country's new leaders. Such a program will be filled out in the weeks ahead as, after appropriate study, I shall submit additional recommendations for your consideration. Today can provide only a sure and substantial beginning.

II.

Our country has come through a painful period of trial and disillusionment since the victory of 1945. We anticipated a world of peace and cooperation. The calculated pressures of aggressive communism have forced us, instead, to live in a world of turmoil.

From this costly experience we have learned one clear lesson. We have learned that the free world cannot indefinitely remain in a posture of paralyzed tension, leaving forever to the aggressor the choice of time and place and means to cause greatest hurt to us at least cost to himself.

This administration has, therefore, begun the definition of a new, positive foreign policy. This policy will be governed by certain fixed ideas. They are these:

(1) Our foreign policy must be clear, consistent, and confident. This means that it must be the product of genuine, continuous cooperation between the executive and the legislative branches of this Government. It must be developed and

directed in the spirit of true bipartisanship.

(2) The policy we embrace must be a coherent global policy. The freedom we cherish and defend in Europe and in the Americas is no different from the freedom that is imperiled in Asia.

(3) Our policy, dedicated to making the free world secure, will envision all peaceful methods and devices—except breaking faith with our friends. We shall never acquiesce in the enslavement of any people in order to purchase fancied gain for ourselves. I shall ask the Congress at a later date to join in an appropriate resolution making clear that this Government recognizes no kind of commitment contained in secret understandings of the past with foreign governments which permit this kind of enslavement.

(4) The policy we pursue will recognize the truth that no single country, even one so powerful as ours, can alone defend the liberty of all nations threatened by Communist aggression from without or subversion within. Mutual security means effective mutual cooperation. For the United States, this means that, as a matter of common sense and national interest, we shall give help to other nations in the measure that they strive earnestly to do their full share of the common task. No wealth of aid could compensate for poverty of spirit. The heart of every free nation must be honestly dedicated to the preserving of its own independence and security.

(5) Our policy will be designed to foster the advent of practical unity in Western Europe. The nations of that region have contributed notably to the effort of sustaining the security of the free world. From the jungles of Indochina and Malaya to the northern shores of Europe, they have vastly improved their defensive strength. Where called upon to do so, they have made costly and bitter sacrifices to hold the line of freedom.

But the problem of security demands closer cooperation among the nations of Europe than has been known to date. Only a more closely integrated economic and political system can provide the greatly increased economic strength needed to maintain both necessary military readiness and respectable living standards.

Europe's enlightened leaders have long been aware of these facts. All the devoted work that has gone into the Schuman plan, the European Army, and the Strasbourg Conference has testified to their vision and determination. These achievements are the more remarkable when we realize that each of them has marked a victory—for France and for Germany alike over the divisions that in the past have brought such tragedy to these two great nations and to the world.

The needed unity of Western Europe manifestly cannot be manufactured from without; it can only be created from within. But it is right and necessary that we encourage Europe's leaders by informing them of the high value we place upon the earnestness of their efforts toward this goal. Real progress will be conclusive evidence to the American people that our material sacrifices in the cause of collective security are matched by essential political, economic, and military accomplishments in Western Europe.

(6) Our foreign policy will recognize the importance of profitable and equitable world trade.

A substantial beginning can and should be made by our friends themselves. Europe, for example, is now marked by checkered areas of labor surplus and labor shortage, of agricultural areas needing machines and industrial areas needing food. Here and elsewhere we can hope that our friends will take the initiative in creating broader markets and more dependable currencies, to allow greater exchange of goods and services among themselves.

Action along these lines can create an economic environment that will invite vital help from us.

This help includes:

First: Revising our customs regulations to remove procedural obstacles to profitable trade. I further recommend that the Congress take the Reciprocal Trade Agreements Act under immediate study and extend it by appropriate legislation. This objective must not ignore legitimate safeguarding of domestic industries, agriculture, and labor standards. In all executive study and recommendations on this problem labor and management and farmers alike will be earnestly consulted.

Second: Doing whatever Government properly can to encourage the flow of private American investment abroad. This involves, as a serious and explicit purpose of our foreign policy, the encouragement of a hospitable climate for such investment in foreign nations.

Third: Availing ourselves of facilities overseas for the economical production of manufactured articles which are needed for mutual defense and which are not seriously competitive with our own normal peacetime production.

Fourth: Receiving from the rest of the world, in equitable exchange for what we supply, greater amounts of important raw materials which we do not ourselves possess in adequate quantities.

III.

In this general discussion of our foreign policy, I must make special mention of the war in Korea.

This war is, for Americans, the most painful phase of Communist aggression throughout the world. It is clearly a part of the same calculated assault that the aggressor is simultaneously pressing in Indochina and in Malaya, and of the strategic situation that manifestly embraces the island of Formosa and the Chinese Nationalist forces there. The working out of any military solution to the Korean war will inevitably affect all these areas.

The administration is giving immediate increased attention to the development of additional Republic of Korea forces. The citizens of that country have proved their capacity as fighting men and their eagerness to take a greater share in the defense of their homeland. Organization, equipment, and training will allow them to do so. Increased assistance to Korea for this purpose conforms fully to our global policies.

In June 1950, following the aggressive attack on the Republic of Korea, the United States Seventh Fleet was instructed both to prevent attack upon Formosa and also to insure that Formosa should not be used as a base of operations against the Chinese Communist mainland.

This has meant, in effect, that the United States Navy was required to serve as a defensive arm of Communist China. Regardless of the situation in 1950, since the date of that order the Chinese Communists have invaded Korea to attack the United Nations forces there. They have consistently rejected the proposals of the United Nations Command for an armistice. They recently joined with Soviet Russia in rejecting the armistice proposal sponsored in the United Nations by the Government of India. This proposal had been accepted by the United States and 53 other nations.

Consequently there is no longer any logic or sense in a condition that required the United States Navy to assume defensive responsibilities on behalf of the Chinese Communists, thus permitting those Communists, with greater impunity, to kill our soldiers and those of our United Nations allies in Korea.

I am, therefore, issuing instructions that the Seventh Fleet no longer be employed to shield Communist China. This order implies no aggressive intent on our part. But we certainly have no obligation to protect a nation fighting us in Korea.

IV.

Our labor for peace in Korea and in the world imperatively demands the maintenance by the United States of a strong fighting service ready for any contingency.

Our problem is to achieve adequate military strength within the limits of endurable strain upon our economy. To amass military power without regard to our economic capacity would be to defend ourselves against one kind of disaster by inviting another.

Both military and economic objectives demand a single national military policy, proper coordination of our armed services, and effective consolidation of certain logistics activities.

We must eliminate waste and duplication of effort in the armed services.

We must realize clearly that size alone is not sufficient. The biggest force is not necessarily the best—and we want the best.

We must not let traditions or habits of the past stand in the way of developing an efficient military force. All members of our forces must be ever mindful that they serve under a single flag and for a single cause.

We must effectively integrate our armament programs and plan them in such careful relation to our industrial facilities that we assure the best use of our manpower and our materials.

Because of the complex technical nature of our military organization and because of the security reasons involved, the Secretary of Defense must take the initiative and assume the responsibility for developing plans to give our Nation maximum safety at minimum cost. Accordingly, the new Secretary of Defense and his civilian and military associates will, in the future, recommend such changes in present laws affecting our defense activities as may be necessary to clarify responsibilities and improve the total effectiveness of our defense effort.

This effort must always conform to policies laid down in the National Security Council.

The statutory function of the National Security Council is to assist the President in the formulation and coordination of significant domestic, foreign, and military policies required for the security of the Nation. In these days of tension it is essential that this central body have the vitality to perform effectively its statutory role. I propose to see that it does so.

Careful formulation of policies must be followed by clear understanding of them by all peoples. A related need, therefore, is to make more effective all activities of the Government related to international information.

I have recently appointed a committee of representative and informed citizens to survey this subject and to make recommendations in the near future for legislative, administrative, or other action.

A unified and dynamic effort in this whole field is essential to the security of the United States and of the other peoples in the community of free nations. There is but one sure way to avoid total war—and that is to win the cold war.

While retaliatory power is one strong deterrent to a would-be aggressor, another powerful deterrent is defensive power. No enemy is likely to attempt an attack foredoomed to failure.

Because the building of a completely impenetrable defense against attack is still not possible, total defensive strength must include civil defense preparedness. Because we have incontrovertible evidence that Soviet Russia possesses atomic weapons, this kind of protection becomes sheer necessity.

Civil defense responsibilities primarily belong to the State and local governments—recruiting, training, and organizing volunteers to meet any emergency. The immediate job of the Federal Government is to provide leadership, to supply technical guidance, and to continue to strengthen its civil defense stockpile of medical, engineering, and related supplies and equipment. This work must go forward without lag.

V.

I have referred to the inescapable need for economic health and strength if we are to maintain adequate military power and exert influential leadership for peace in the world.

Our immediate task is to chart a fiscal and economic policy that can:

(1) Reduce the planned deficits and then balance the budget, which means, among other things, reducing Federal expenditures to the safe minimum;

(2) Meet the huge costs of our defense;

(3) Properly handle the burden of our inheritance of debt and obligations;

(4) Check the menace of inflation;

(5) Work toward the earliest possible reduction of the tax burden;

(6) Make constructive plans to encourage the initiative of our citizens.

It is important that all of us understand that this administration does not and cannot begin its task with a clean slate. Much already has been written on the record, beyond our power quickly to erase or to amend. This record includes our inherited burden of indebtedness and obligations and deficits.

The current year's budget, as you know, carries a 5.9 billion dollar deficit; and the budget, which was presented to you before this administration took office, indicates a budgetary deficit of 9.9 billion for the fiscal year ending June 30, 1954. The national debt is now more than 265 billion dollars. In addition, the accumulated obligational authority of the Federal Government for future payment totals over 80 billion dollars. Even this amount is exclusive of large contingent liabilities, so numerous and extensive as to be almost beyond description.

The bills for the payment of nearly all of the 80 billion dollars of obligations will be presented during the next 4 years. These bills, added to the current costs of government we must meet, make a formidable burden.

The present authorized Government-debt limit is 275 billion dollars. The forecast presented by the outgoing administration with the fiscal year 1954 budget indicates that—before the end of the fiscal year and at the peak of demand for payments during the year—the total Government debt may approach and even exceed that limit. Unless budgeted deficits are checked, the momentum of past programs will force an increase of the statutory debt limit.

Permit me this one understatement: to meet and to correct this situation will not be easy.

Permit me this one assurance: every department head and I are determined to do everything we can to resolve it.

The first order of business is the elimination of the annual deficit. This cannot be achieved merely by exhortation. It demands the concerted action of all those in responsible positions in the Government and the earnest cooperation of the

Congress.

Already, we have begun an examination of the appropriations and expenditures of all departments in an effort to find significant items that may be decreased or canceled without damage to our essential requirements.

Getting control of the budget requires also that State and local governments and interested groups of citizens restrain themselves in their demands upon the Congress that the Federal Treasury spend more and more money for all types of projects.

A balanced budget is an essential first measure in checking further depreciation in the buying power of the dollar. This is one of the critical steps to be taken to bring an end to planned inflation. Our purpose is to manage the Government's finances so as to help and not hinder each family in balancing its own budget.

Reduction of taxes will be justified only as we show we can succeed in bringing the budget under control. As the budget is balanced and inflation checked, the tax burden that today stifles initiative can and must be eased.

Until we can determine the extent to which expenditures can be reduced, it would not be wise to reduce our revenues.

Meanwhile, the tax structure as a whole demands review. The Secretary of the Treasury is undertaking this study immediately. We must develop a system of taxation which will impose the least possible obstacle to the dynamic growth of the country. This includes particularly real opportunity for the growth of small businesses. Many readjustments in existing taxes will be necessary to serve these objectives and also to remove existing inequities. Clarification and simplification in the tax laws as well as the regulations will be undertaken.

In the entire area of fiscal policy—which must, in its various aspects, be treated in recommendations to the Congress in coming weeks—there can now be stated certain basic facts and principles.

First. It is axiomatic that our economy is a highly complex and sensitive mechanism. Hasty and ill-considered action of any kind could seriously upset the subtle equation that encompasses debts, obligations, expenditures, defense demands, deficits, taxes, and the general economic health of the Nation. Our goals can be clear, our start toward them can be immediate—but action must be gradual.

Second. It is clear that too great a part of the national debt comes due in too short a time. The Department of the Treasury will undertake at suitable times a program of extending part of the debt over longer periods and gradually placing greater amounts in the hands of longer-term investors.

Third. Past differences in policy between the Treasury and the Federal Reserve Board have helped to encourage inflation. Henceforth, I expect that their single purpose shall be to serve the whole Nation by policies designed to stabilize the economy and encourage the free play of our people's genius for individual initiative.

In encouraging this initiative, no single item in our current problems has received more thoughtful consideration by my associates, and by the many individuals called into our counsels, than the matter of price and wage control by law.

The great economic strength of our democracy has developed in an atmosphere of freedom. The character of our people resists artificial and arbitrary controls of any kind. Direct controls, except those on credit, deal not with the real causes of inflation but only with its symptoms. In times of national emergency, this kind of control has a role to play. Our whole system, however, is based upon the assumption that, normally, we should combat wide fluctuations in our price structure by relying largely on the effective use of sound fiscal and monetary policy, and upon the natural workings of economic law.

Moreover, American labor and American business can best resolve their wage problems across the bargaining table. Government should refrain from sitting in with them unless, in extreme cases, the public welfare requires protection.

We are, of course, living in an international situation that is neither an emergency demanding full mobilization, nor is it peace. No one can know how long this condition will persist. Consequently, we are forced to learn many new things as we go along-clinging to what works, discarding what does not.

In all our current discussions on these and related facts, the weight of evidence is clearly against the use of controls in their present forms. They have proved largely unsatisfactory or unworkable. They have not prevented inflation; they have not kept down the cost of living. Dissatisfaction with them is wholly justified. I am convinced that now—as well as in the long run—free and competitive prices will best serve the interests of all the people, and best meet the changing, growing needs of our economy.

Accordingly, I do not intend to ask for a renewal of the present wage and price controls on April 30, 1953, when present legislation expires. In the meantime, steps will be taken to eliminate controls in an orderly manner, and to terminate special agencies no longer needed for this purpose. It is obviously to be expected that the removal of these controls will result in individual price changes—some up, some down. But a maximum of freedom in market prices as well as in collective bargaining is characteristic of a truly free people.

I believe also that material and product controls should be ended, except with respect to defense priorities and scarce and critical items essential for our defense. I shall recommend to the Congress that legislation be enacted to continue authority for such remaining controls of this type as will be necessary after the expiration of the existing statute on June 30, 1953.

I recommend the continuance of the authority for Federal control over rents in those communities in which serious housing shortages exist. These are chiefly the so-called defense areas. In these and all areas the Federal Government should withdraw from the control of rents as soon as practicable. But before they are removed entirely, each legislature should have full opportunity to take over, within its own State, responsibility for this function.

It would be idle to pretend that all our problems in this whole field of prices will solve themselves by mere Federal withdrawal from direct controls.

We shall have to watch trends closely. If the freer functioning of our economic system, as well as the indirect controls which can be appropriately employed, prove insufficient during this period of strain and tension, I shall promptly ask the Congress to enact such legislation as may be required.

In facing all these problems—wages, prices, production, tax rates, fiscal policy, deficits—everywhere we remain constantly mindful that the time for sacrifice has not ended. But we are concerned with the encouragement of competitive enterprise and individual initiative precisely because we know them to be our Nation's abiding sources of strength.

VI.

Our vast world responsibility accents with urgency our people's elemental right to a government whose clear qualities are loyalty, security, efficiency, economy, and integrity.

The safety of America and the trust of the people alike demand that the personnel of the Federal Government be loyal in their motives and reliable in the discharge of their duties. Only a combination of both loyalty and reliability promises genuine security.

To state this principle is easy; to apply it can be difficult. But this security we must and shall have. By way of example, all principal new appointees to departments and agencies have been investigated at their own request by the Federal Bureau of Investigation.

Confident of your understanding and cooperation, I know that the primary responsibility for keeping out the disloyal and the dangerous rests squarely upon the executive branch. When this branch so conducts itself as to require policing by another branch of the Government, it invites its own disorder and confusion.

I am determined to meet this responsibility of the Executive. The heads of all executive departments and agencies have been instructed to initiate at once effective programs of security with respect to their personnel. The Attorney General will advise and guide the departments and agencies in the shaping of these programs, designed at once to govern the employment of new personnel and to review speedily any derogatory information concerning incumbent personnel.

To carry out these programs, I believe that the powers of the executive branch under existing law are sufficient. If they should prove inadequate, the necessary legislation will be requested.

These programs will be both fair to the rights of the individual and effective for the safety of the Nation. They will, with care and justice, apply the basic principle that public employment is not a right but a privilege.

All these measures have two clear purposes: Their first purpose is to make certain that this Nation's security is not jeopardized by false servants. Their second purpose is to clear the atmosphere of that unreasoned suspicion that accepts rumor and gossip as substitutes for evidence.

Our people, of course, deserve and demand of their Federal Government more than security of personnel. They demand, also, efficient and logical organization, true to constitutional principles.

I have already established a Committee on Government Organization. The Committee is using as its point of departure the reports of the Hoover Commission and subsequent studies by several independent agencies. To achieve the greater efficiency and economy which the Committee analyses show to be possible, I ask the Congress to extend the present Government Reorganization Act for a period of 18 months or 2 years beyond its expiration date of April 1, 1953.

There is more involved here than realigning the wheels and smoothing the gears of administrative machinery. The Congress rightfully-expects the Executive to take the initiative in discovering and removing outmoded functions and eliminating duplication.

One agency, for example, whose head has promised early and vigorous action to provide greater efficiency is the Post Office. One of the oldest institutions of our Federal Government, its service should be of the best. Its employees should merit and receive the high regard and esteem of the citizens of the Nation. There are today in some areas of the postal service, both waste and incompetence to be corrected. With the cooperation of the Congress, and taking advantage of its accumulated experience in postal affairs, the Postmaster General will institute a program directed at improving service while at the same time reducing costs and decreasing deficits.

In all departments, dedication to these basic precepts of security and efficiency, integrity, and economy can and will produce an administration deserving of the trust the people have placed in it.

Our people have demanded nothing less than good, efficient government. They shall get nothing less.

VII.

Vitally important are the water and minerals, public lands and standing timber, forage and Mid-life of this country. A fast-growing population will have vast future needs in these resources. We must more than match the substantial achievements in the half-century since President Theodore Roosevelt awakened the Nation to the problem of conservation.

This calls for a strong Federal program in the field of resource development. Its major projects should be timed, where possible to assist in leveling off peaks and valleys in our economic life. Soundly planned projects already initiated should be carried out. New ones will be planned for the future.

The best natural resources program for America will not result from exclusive dependence on Federal bureaucracy. It will involve a partnership of the States and local communities, private citizens, and the Federal Government, all working together. This combined effort will advance the development of the great river valleys of our Nation and the power that they can generate. Likewise, such a partnership can be effective in the expansion throughout the Nation of upstream storage; the sound use of public lands; the wise conservation of minerals; and the sustained yield of our forests.

There has been much criticism, some of it apparently justified, of the confusion resulting from overlapping Federal activities in the entire field of resource-conservation. This matter is being exhaustively studied and appropriate reorganization plans will be developed.

Most of these particular resource problems pertain to the Department of the Interior. Another of its major concerns is our country's island possessions. Here, one matter deserves attention. The platforms of both political parties promised immediate statehood to Hawaii. The people of that Territory have earned that status. Statehood should be granted promptly with the first election scheduled for 1954.

VIII.

One of the difficult problems which face the new administration is that of the slow, irregular decline of farm prices. This decline, which has been going on for almost 2 years, has occurred at a time when most nonfarm prices and farm costs of production are extraordinarily high.

Present agricultural legislation provides for the mandatory support of the prices of basic farm commodities at 90 percent of parity. The Secretary of Agriculture and his associates will, of course, execute the present act faithfully and thereby seek to mitigate the consequences of the downturn in farm income.

This price-support legislation will expire at the end of 1954.

So we should begin now to consider what farm legislation we should develop for 1955 and beyond. Our aim should be economic stability and full parity of income for American farmers. But we must seek this goal in ways that minimize governmental interference in the farmers' affairs, that permit desirable shifts in production, and that encourage farmers themselves to use initiative in meeting changing economic conditions.

A continuing study reveals nothing more emphatically than the complicated nature of this subject. Among other things, it shows that the prosperity of our agriculture depends directly upon the prosperity of the whole country—upon the purchasing power of American consumers. It depends also upon the opportunity to ship abroad large surpluses of particular commodities, and therefore upon sound economic relationships between the United States and many foreign countries. It involves research and scientific investigation, conducted on an extensive scale. It involves special credit mechanisms and marketing, rural electrification, soil conservation, and other programs.

The whole complex of agricultural programs and policies will be studied by a Special Agricultural Advisory Commission, as I know it will by appropriate committees of the Congress. A nonpartisan group of respected authorities in the field of agriculture has already been appointed as an interim advisory group.

The immediate changes needed in agricultural programs are largely budgetary and administrative in nature. New policies and new programs must await the completion of the far-reaching studies which have already been launched.

IX.

The determination of labor policy must be governed not by the vagaries of political expediency but by the firmest principles and convictions. Slanted partisan appeals to American workers, spoken as if they were a group apart, necessitating a special language and treatment, are an affront to the fullness of their dignity as American citizens.

The truth in matters of labor policy has become obscured in controversy. The very meaning of economic freedom as it affects labor has become confused. This misunderstanding has provided a climate of opinion favoring the growth of governmental paternalism in labor relations. This tendency, if left uncorrected, could end only by producing a bureaucratic despotism. Economic freedom is, in fact, the requisite of greater prosperity for every American who earns his own living.

In the field of labor legislation, only a law that merits the respect and support of both labor and management can help reduce the loss of wages and of production through strikes and stoppages, and thus add to the total economic strength of our Nation.

We have now had 5 years' experience with the Labor Management Act of 1947, commonly known as the Taft-Hartley Act. That experience has shown the need for some corrective action, and we should promptly proceed to amend that act.

I know that the Congress is already proceeding with renewed studies of this subject. Meanwhile, the Department of Labor is at once beginning work to devise further specific recommendations for your consideration.

In the careful working out of legislation, I know you will give thoughtful consideration—as will we in the executive branch—to the views of labor, and of management, and of the general public. In this process, it is only human that each of us should bring forward the arguments of self-interest. But if all conduct their arguments in the overpowering light of national interest—which is enlightened self-interest—we shall get the right answers. I profoundly hope that every citizen of our country will follow with understanding your progress in this work. The welfare of all of us is involved.

Especially must we remember that the institutions of trade unionism and collective bargaining are monuments to the freedom that must prevail in our industrial life. They have a century of honorable achievement behind them. Our faith in them is proven, firm, and final.

Government can do a great deal to aid the settlement of labor disputes without allowing itself to be employed as an ally of either side. Its proper role in industrial strife is to encourage the processes of mediation and conciliation. These processes can successfully be directed only by a government free from the taint of any suspicion that it is partial or punitive.

The administration intends to strengthen and to improve the services which the Department of Labor can render to the worker and to the whole national community. This Department was created—just 40 years ago—to serve the entire Nation. It must aid, for example, employers and employees alike in improving training programs that will develop skilled and competent workers. It must enjoy the confidence and respect of labor and industry in order to play a significant role in the planning of America's economic future. To that end, I am authorizing the Department of Labor to establish promptly a tripartite advisory committee consisting of representatives of employers, labor, and the public.

X.

Our civil and social rights form a central part of the heritage we are striving to defend on all fronts and with all our strength. I believe with all my heart that our vigilant guarding of these rights is a sacred obligation binding upon every citizen. To be true to one's own freedom is, in essence, to honor and respect the freedom of all others.

A cardinal ideal in this heritage we cherish is the equality of rights of all citizens of every race and color and creed.

We know that discrimination against minorities persists despite our allegiance to this ideal. Such discrimination—confined to no one section of the Nation—is but the outward testimony to the persistence of distrust and of fear in the hearts of men.

This fact makes all the more vital the fighting of these wrongs by each individual, in every station of life, in his every deed.

Much of the answer lies in the power of fact, fully publicized; of persuasion, honestly pressed; and of conscience, justly aroused. These are methods familiar to our way of life, tested and proven wise.

I propose to use whatever authority exists in the office of the President to end segregation in the District of Columbia, including the Federal Government, and any segregation in the Armed Forces.

Here in the District of Columbia, serious attention should be given to the proposal to develop and authorize, through legislation, a system to provide an effective voice in local self-government. While consideration of this proceeds, I recommend an immediate increase of two in the number of District Commissioners to broaden representation of all elements of our local population. This will be a first step toward insuring that this Capital provide an honored example to all communities of our Nation.

In this manner, and by the leadership of the office of the President exercised through friendly conferences with those in authority in our States and cities, we expect to make true and rapid progress in civil rights and equality of employment opportunity.

There is one sphere in which civil rights are inevitably involved in Federal legislation. This is the sphere of immigration.

It is a manifest right of our Government to limit the number of immigrants our Nation can absorb. It is also a manifest right of our Government to set reasonable requirements on the character and the numbers of the people who come to share our land and our freedom.

It is well for us, however, to remind ourselves occasionally of an equally manifest fact: we are—one and all—immigrants or sons and daughters of immigrants.

Existing legislation contains injustices. It does, in fact, discriminate. I am informed by Members of the Congress that it was realized, at the time of its enactment, that future study of the basis of determining quotas would be necessary.

I am therefore requesting the Congress to review this legislation and to enact a statute that will at one and the same time guard our legitimate national interests and be faithful to our basic ideas of freedom and fairness to all.

In another but related area—that of social rights—we see most clearly the new application of old ideas of freedom.

This administration is profoundly aware of two great needs born of our living in a complex industrial economy. First, the individual citizen must have safeguards against personal disaster inflicted by forces beyond his control; second, the welfare of the people demands effective and economical performance by the Government of certain indispensable social services.

In the light of this responsibility, certain general purposes and certain concrete measures are plainly indicated now.

There is urgent need for greater effectiveness in our programs, both public and private, offering safeguards against the privations that too often come with unemployment, old age, illness, and accident. The provisions of the old-age and survivors insurance law should promptly be extended to cover millions of citizens who have been left out of the social-security system. No less important is the encouragement of privately sponsored pension plans. Most important of all, of course, is renewed effort to check the inflation which destroys so much of the value of all social-security payments.

Our school system demands some prompt, effective help. During each of the last 9 years, more than 1 S million children have swelled the elementary and secondary school population of the country. Generally, the school population is proportionately higher in States with low per capita income. This whole situation calls for careful congressional study and action. I am sure that you share my conviction that the firm conditions of Federal aid must be proved need and proved lack of local income.

One phase of the school problem demands special action. The school population of many districts has been greatly increased by the swift growth of defense activities. These activities have added little or nothing to the tax resources of the communities affected. Legislation aiding construction of schools in the districts expires on June 30. This law should be renewed; and likewise, the partial payments for current operating expenses for these particular school districts should be made, including the deficiency requirement of the current fiscal year.

Public interest similarly demands one prompt specific action in protection of the general consumer. The Food and Drug Administration should be authorized to continue its established and necessary program of factory inspections. The invalidation of these inspections by the Supreme Court of December 8, 1952, was based solely on the fact that the present law contained inconsistent and unclear provisions. These must be promptly corrected.

I am well aware that beyond these few immediate measures there remains much to be done. The health and housing needs of our people call for intelligently planned programs. Involved are the solvency of the whole security system; and its guarding against exploitation by the irresponsible.

To bring clear purpose and orderly procedure into this field, I anticipate a thorough study of the proper relationship among Federal, State, and local programs. I shall shortly send you specific recommendations for establishing such an appropriate commission, together with a reorganization plan defining new administrative status for all Federal activities in health, education, and social security.

I repeat that there are many important subjects of which I make no mention today. Among these is our great and growing body of veterans. America has traditionally been generous in caring for the disabled—and the widow and the orphan of the fallen. These millions remain close to all our hearts. Proper care of our uniformed citizens and appreciation of the past service of our veterans are part of our accepted governmental responsibilities.

XI

We have surveyed briefly some problems of our people and a portion of the tasks before us.

The hope of freedom itself depends, in real measure, upon our strength, our heart, and our wisdom.

We must be strong in arms. We must be strong in the source of all our armament, our productivity. We all—workers and farmers, foremen and financiers, technicians and builders—all must produce, produce more, and produce yet more.

We must be strong, above all, in the spiritual resources upon which all else depends. We must be devoted with all our heart to the values we defend. We must know that each of these values and virtues applies with equal force at the ends of the earth and in our relations with our neighbor next door. We must know that freedom expresses itself with equal eloquence in the right of workers to strike in the nearby factory, and in the yearnings and sufferings of the peoples of Eastern Europe.

As our heart summons our strength, our wisdom must direct it.

There is, in world affairs, a steady course to be followed between an assertion of strength that is truculent and a confession of helplessness that is cowardly.

There is, in our affairs at home, a middle way between untrammeled freedom of the individual and the demands for the welfare of the whole Nation. This way must avoid government by bureaucracy as carefully as it avoids neglect of the helpless.

In every area of political action, free men must think before they can expect to win.

In this spirit must we live and labor: confident of our strength, compassionate in our heart, clear in our mind.

In this spirit, let us together turn to the great tasks before us.

2.2 Dwight D. Eisenhower's Second State of the Union Address

Mr. President, Mr. Speaker, Members of the Eighty-third Congress:

It is a high honor again to present to the Congress my views on the state of the Union and to recommend measures to advance the security, prosperity, and well-being of the American people.

All branches of this Government—and I venture to say both of our great parties—can support the general objective of the recommendations I make today, for that objective is the building of a stronger America. A nation whose every citizen has good reason for bold hope; where effort is rewarded and prosperity is shared; where freedom expands and peace is secure—that is what I mean by a stronger America.

Toward this objective a real momentum has been developed during this Administration's first year in office. We mean to continue that momentum and to increase it. We mean to build a better future for this nation.

Much for which we may be thankful has happened during the past year.

First of all we are deeply grateful that our sons no longer die on the distant mountains of Korea. Although they are still called from our homes to military service, they are no longer called to the field of battle.

The nation has just completed the most prosperous year in its history. The damaging effect of inflation on the wages, pensions, salaries and savings of us all has been brought under control. Taxes have begun to go down. The cost of our government has been reduced and its work proceeds with some 183,000 fewer employees; thus the discouraging trend of modern governments toward their own limitless expansion has in our case been reversed. The cost of armaments becomes less oppressive as we near our defense goals; yet we are militarily stronger every day. During the year, creation of the new Cabinet Department of Health, Education, and Welfare symbolized the government's permanent concern with the human problems of our citizens.

Segregation in the armed forces and other Federal activities is on the way out. We have also made progress toward its elimination in the District of Columbia. These are steps in the continuing effort to eliminate inter-racial difficulty.

Some developments beyond our shores have been equally encouraging. Communist aggression, halted in Korea, continues to meet in Indo-china the vigorous resistance of France and the Associated States, assisted by timely aid from our country. In West Germany, in Iran, and in other areas of the world, heartening political victories have been won by the forces of stability and freedom. Slowly but surely, the free world gathers strength. Meanwhile, from behind the iron curtain, there are signs that tyranny is in trouble and reminders that its structure is as brittle as its surface is hard.

There has been in fact a great strategic change in the world during the past year. That precious intangible, the initiative, is becoming ours. Our policy, not limited to mere reaction against crises provoked by others, is free to develop along lines of our choice not only abroad, but also at home. As a major theme for American policy during the coming year, let our joint determination be to hold this new initiative and to use it.

We shall use this initiative to promote three broad purposes: First, to protect the freedom of our people; second, to maintain a strong, growing economy; third, to concern ourselves with the human problems of the individual citizen.

Only by active concern for each of these purposes can we be sure that we are on the forward road to a better and a stronger America. All my recommendations today are in furtherance of these three purposes.

I. FOREIGN AFFAIRS

American freedom is threatened so long as the world Communist conspiracy exists in its present scope, power and hostility. More closely than ever before, American freedom is interlocked with the freedom of other people. In the unity of the free world lies our best chance to reduce the Communist threat without war. In the task of maintaining this unity and strengthening all its parts, the greatest responsibility falls naturally on those who, like ourselves, retain the most freedom and strength.

We shall, therefore, continue to advance the cause of freedom on foreign fronts.

In the Far East, we retain our vital interest in Korea. We have negotiated with the Republic of Korea a mutual security pact, which develops our security system for the Pacific and which I shall promptly submit to the Senate for its consent to ratification. We are prepared to meet any renewal of armed aggression in Korea. We shall maintain indefinitely our bases in Okinawa. I shall ask the Congress to authorize continued material assistance to hasten the successful conclusion of the struggle in Indo-china. This assistance will also bring closer the day when the Associated States may enjoy the independence already assured by France. We shall also continue military and economic aid to the Nationalist Government of China.

In South Asia, profound changes are taking place in free nations which are demonstrating their ability to progress through democratic methods. They provide an inspiring contrast to the dictatorial methods and backward course of events in Communist China. In these continuing efforts, the free peoples of South Asia can be assured of the support of the United States.

In the Middle East, where tensions and serious problems exist, we will show sympathetic and impartial friendship.

In Western Europe our policy rests firmly on the North Atlantic Treaty. It will remain so based as far ahead as we can see. Within its organization, the building of a united European community, including France and Germany, is vital to a free and self-reliant Europe. This will be promoted by the European Defense Community which offers assurance of European security. With the coming of unity to Western Europe, the assistance this Nation can render for the security of Europe and the free world will be multiplied in effectiveness.

In the Western Hemisphere we shall continue to develop harmonious and mutually beneficial cooperation with our neighbors. Indeed, solid friendship with all our American neighbors is a cornerstone of our entire policy.

In the world as a whole, the United Nations, admittedly still in a state of evolution, means much to the United States. It has given uniquely valuable services in many places where violence threatened. It is the only real world forum where we have the opportunity for international presentation and rebuttal. It is a place where the nations of the world can, if they have the will, take collective action for peace and justice. It is a place where the guilt can be squarely assigned to those who fail to take all necessary steps to keep the peace. The United Nations deserves our continued firm support.

FOREIGN ASSISTANCE AND TRADE

In the practical application of our foreign policy, we enter the field of foreign assistance and trade.

Military assistance must be continued. Technical assistance must be maintained. Economic assistance can be reduced. However, our economic programs in Korea and in a few other critical places of the world are especially important, and I shall ask Congress to continue them in the next fiscal year.

The forthcoming Budget Message will propose maintenance of the Presidential power of transferability of all assistance funds and will ask authority to merge these funds with the regular defense funds. It will also propose that the Secretary of Defense have primary responsibility for the administration of foreign military assistance in accordance with the policy guidance of the Secretary of State.

The fact that we can now reduce our foreign economic assistance in many areas is gratifying evidence that its objectives are being achieved. By continuing to surpass her prewar levels of economic activity, Western Europe gains self-reliance. Thus our relationship enters a new phase which can bring results beneficial to our taxpayers and our allies alike, if still another step is taken.

This step is the creation of a healthier and freer system of trade and payments within the free world—a system in which our allies can earn their own way and our own economy can continue to flourish. The free world can no longer afford the kinds of arbitrary restraints on trade that have continued ever since the war. On this problem I shall submit to the Congress detailed recommendations, after our Joint Commission on Foreign Economic Policy has made its report.

ATOMIC ENERGY PROPOSAL

As we maintain our military strength during the coming year and draw closer the bonds with our allies, we shall be in an improved position to discuss outstanding issues with the Soviet Union. Indeed we shall be glad to do so whenever there is a reasonable prospect of constructive results. In this spirit the atomic energy proposals of the United States were recently presented to the United Nations General Assembly. A truly constructive Soviet reaction will make possible a new start toward an era of peace, and away from the fatal road toward atomic war.

DEFENSE

Since our hope is peace, we owe ourselves and the world a candid explanation of the military measures we are taking to make that peace secure.

As we enter this new year, our military power continues to grow. This power is for our own defense and to deter aggression.

We shall not be aggressors, but we and our allies have and will maintain a massive capability to strike back.

Here are some of the considerations in our defense planning:

First, while determined to use atomic power to serve the usages of peace, we take into full account our great and growing number of nuclear weapons and the most effective means of using them against an aggressor if they are needed to preserve our freedom. Our defense will be stronger if, under appropriate security safeguards, we share with our allies certain knowledge of the tactical use of our nuclear weapons. I urge the Congress to provide the needed authority.

Second, the usefulness of these new weapons creates new relationships between men and materials. These new relationships permit economies in the use of men as we build forces suited to our situation in the world today. As will be seen from the Budget Message on January 21, the airpower of our Navy and Air Force is receiving heavy emphasis.

Third, our armed forces must regain maximum mobility of action. Our strategic reserves must be centrally placed and readily deployable to meet sudden aggression against ourselves and our allies.

Fourth, our defense must rest on trained manpower and its most economical and mobile use. A professional corps is the heart of any security organization. It is necessarily the teacher and leader of those who serve temporarily in the discharge of the obligation to help defend the Republic. Pay alone will not retain in the career service of our armed forces the necessary numbers of long-term personnel. I strongly urge, therefore, a more generous use of other benefits important to service morale. Among these are more adequate living quarters and family housing units and medical care for dependents.

Studies of military manpower have just been completed by the National Security Training Commission and a Committee appointed by the Director of the Office of Defense Mobilization. Evident weaknesses exist in the state of readiness and organization of our reserve forces. Measures to correct these weaknesses will be later submitted to the Congress.

Fifth, the ability to convert swiftly from partial to all-out mobilization is imperative to our security. For the first time, mobilization officials know what the requirements are for 1,000 major items needed for military uses. These data, now being related to civilian requirements and our supply potential, will show us the gaps in our mobilization base. Thus we shall have more realistic plant-expansion and stockpiling goals. We shall speed their attainment. This Nation is at last to have an up-to-date mobilization base—the foundation of a sound defense program.

Another part of this foundation is, of course, our continental transport system. Some of our vital heavy materials come increasingly from Canada. Indeed our relations with Canada, happily always close, involve more and more the unbreakable ties of strategic interdependence. Both nations now need the St. Lawrence Seaway for security as well as for economic reasons. I urge the Congress promptly to approve our participation in its construction.

Sixth, military and non-military measures for continental defense must be and are being strengthened. In the current fiscal year we are allocating to these purposes an increasing portion of our effort, and in the next fiscal year we shall spend nearly a billion dollars more for them than in 1953.

An indispensable part of our continental security is our civil defense effort. This will succeed only as we have the complete cooperation of State Governors, Mayors, and voluntary citizen groups. With their help we can advance a cooperative program which, if an attack should come, would save many lives and lessen destruction.

The defense program recommended in the 1955 Budget is consistent with all of the considerations which I have just discussed. It is based on a new military program unanimously recommended by the Joint Chiefs of Staff and approved by me following consideration by the National Security Council. This new program will make and keep America strong in an age of peril. Nothing should bar its attainment.

The international and defense policies which I have outlined will enable us to negotiate from a position of strength as we hold our resolute course toward a peaceful world. We now turn to matters which are normally characterized as domestic, well realizing that what we do abroad affects every problem at home—from the amount of taxes to our very state of mind.

INTERNAL SECURITY

Under the standards established for the new employee security program, more than 2,200 employees have been separated from the Federal government. Our national security demands that the investigation of new employees and the evaluation of derogatory information respecting present employees be expedited and concluded at the earliest possible date. I shall recommend that the Congress provide additional funds where necessary to speed these important procedures.

From the special employment standards of the Federal government I turn now to a matter relating to American citizenship. The subversive character of the Communist Party in the United States has been clearly demonstrated in many ways, including court proceedings. We should recognize by law a fact that is plain to all thoughtful citizens-that we are dealing here with actions akin to treason—that when a citizen knowingly participates in the Communist conspiracy he no longer holds allegiance to the United States.

I recommend that Congress enact legislation to provide that a citizen of the United States who is convicted in the courts of hereafter conspiring to advocate the overthrow of this government by force or violence be treated as having, by such act, renounced his allegiance to the United States and forfeited his United States citizenship.

In addition, the Attorney General will soon appear before your Committees to present his recommendations for needed additional legal weapons with which to combat subversion in our country and to deal with the question of claimed immunity.

II. STRONG ECONOMY

I turn now to the second great purpose of our government: Along with the protection of freedom, the maintenance of a strong and growing economy.

The American economy is one of the wonders of the world. It undergirds our international position, our military security, and the standard of living of every citizen. This Administration is determined to keep our economy strong and to keep it growing.

At this moment we are in transition from a wartime to a peacetime economy. I am confident that we can complete this transition without serious interruption in our economic growth. But we shall not leave this vital matter to chance. Economic preparedness is fully as important to the nation as military preparedness.

Subsequent special messages and the economic report on January 28 will set forth plans of the Administration and its recommendations for Congressional action. These will include flexible credit and debt management policies; tax measures to stimulate consumer and business spending; suitable lending, guaranteeing, insuring, and grant-in-aid activities; strengthened old-age and unemployment insurance measures; improved agricultural programs; public-works plans laid well in advance; enlarged opportunities for international trade and investment. This mere enumeration of these subjects implies the vast amount of study, coordination, and planning, to say nothing of authorizing legislation, that altogether make our economic preparedness complete.

If new conditions arise that require additional administrative or legislative action, the Administration will still be ready. A government always ready, as this is, to take well-timed and vigorous action, and a business community willing, as ours is, to plan ,boldly and with confidence, can between them develop a climate assuring steady economic growth.

THE BUDGET

I shall submit to the Congress on January 21 the first budget prepared by this Administration, for the period July 1, 1954, through June 1955. This budget is adequate to the current needs of the government. It recognizes that a Federal budget should be a stabilizing factor in the economy. Its tax and expenditure programs will foster individual initiative and economic growth.

Pending the transmittal of my Budget Message, I shall mention here only a few points about our budgetary situation.

First, one of our initial acts was to revise, with the cooperation of the Congress, the Budget prepared before this Administration took office. Requests for new appropriations were greatly reduced. In addition, the spending level provided in that Budget for the current fiscal year has been reduced by about $7,000,000,000. In the next fiscal year we estimate a further reduction in expenditures of more than $5,000,000,000. This will reduce the spending level over the two fiscal years by more than $12,000,000,000. We are also reducing further our requests for new appropriations.

Second, despite the substantial loss of revenue in the coming fiscal year, resulting from tax reductions now in effect and tax adjustments which I shall propose, our reduced spending will move the new budget closer to a balance.

Third, by keeping new appropriation requests below estimated revenues, we continue to reduce the tremendous accumulation of unfinanced obligations incurred by the Government under past appropriations.

Fourth, until those claims on our Government's revenues are further reduced, the growth in the public debt cannot be entirely stopped. Because of this—because the government's bills have to be paid every month, while the tax money to pay them comes in with great unevenness within the fiscal year—and because of the need for flexibility to manage this enormous debt, I find it necessary to renew my request for an increase in the statutory debt limit.

TAXES

The new budget provides for a lower level of taxation than has prevailed in preceding years. Six days ago individual income taxes were reduced and the excess profits tax expired. These tax reductions are justified only because of the substantial reductions we already have made and are making in governmental expenditures. As additional reductions in expenditures are brought gradually but surely into sight, further reductions in taxes can and will be made. When budget savings and sound governmental financing are assured, tax burdens should be reduced so that taxpayers may spend their own money in their own way.

While we are moving toward lower levels of taxation we must thoroughly revise our whole tax system. The groundwork for this revision has already been laid by the Committee on Ways and Means of the House of Representatives, in close consultation with the Department of the Treasury. We should now remove the more glaring tax inequities, particularly on small taxpayers; reduce restraints on the growth of small business; and make other changes that will encourage initiative, enterprise and production. Twenty-five recommendations toward these ends will be contained in my budget message.

Without attempting to summarize these manifold reforms, I can here illustrate their tendency. For example, we propose more liberal tax treatment for dependent children who work, for widows or widowers with dependent children, and for medical expenses. For the business that wants to expand or modernize its plant, we propose liberalized tax treatment of depreciation, research and development expenses, and retained earnings.

Because of the present need for revenue the corporation income tax should be kept at the current rate of 52% for another year, and the excise taxes scheduled to be reduced on April first, including those on liquor, tobacco, gasoline and automobiles, should be continued at present rates.

Immediate extension of the Renegotiation Act of 1951 is also needed to eliminate excessive profits and to prevent waste of public funds in the purchase of defense materials.

AGRICULTURE

The well being of our 160 million people demands a stable and prosperous agriculture. Conversely, every farmer knows he cannot prosper unless all America prospers. As we seek to promote increases in our standard of living, we must be sure that the farmer fairly shares in that increase. Therefore, a farm program promoting stability and prosperity in all elements of our agriculture is urgently needed.

Agricultural laws now in effect successfully accomplished their wartime purpose of encouraging maximum production of many crops. Today, production of these crops at such levels far exceeds present demand. Yet the laws encouraging such production are still in effect. The storage facilities of the Commodity Credit Corporation bulge with surplus stocks of dairy products, wheat, cotton, corn, and certain vegetable oils; and the Corporation's presently authorized borrowing authority--$6,750,000,000—is nearly exhausted. Some products, priced out of domestic markets, and others, priced out of world markets, have piled up in government hands. In a world in which millions of people are hungry, destruction of food would, of course, be unconscionable. Yet surplus stocks continue to threaten the market and in spite of the acreage controls authorized by present law, surpluses will continue to accumulate.

We confront two alternatives. The first is to impose still greater acreage reductions for some crops and apply rigid Federal controls over the use of the diverted acres. This will regiment the production of every basic agricultural crop. It will place every producer of those crops under the domination and control of the Federal government in Washington. This alternative is contrary to the fundamental interests, not only of the farmer, but of the Nation as a whole. Nor is it a real solution to the problem facing us.

The second alternative is to permit the market price for these agricultural products gradually to have a greater influence on the planning of production by farmers, while continuing the assistance of the government. This is the sound approach. To make it effective, surpluses existing when the new program begins must be insulated from the normal channels of trade for special uses. These uses would include school lunch programs, disaster relief, emergency assistance to foreign friends, and of particular importance the stockpiling of reserves for a national emergency.

Building on the agricultural laws of 1948 and 1949, we should establish a price support program with enough flexibility to attract the production of needed supplies of essential commodities and to stimulate the consumption of those commodities that are flooding American markets. Transition to modernized parity must be accomplished gradually. In no case should there be an abrupt downward change in the dollar level or in the percentage level of price supports.

Next Monday I shall transmit to the Congress my detailed recommendations embodying this approach. They have been developed through the cooperation of innumerable individuals vitally interested in agriculture. My special message on Monday will briefly describe the consultative and advisory processes to which this whole program has been subjected during the past ten months.

I have chosen this farm program because it will build markets, protect the consumers' food supply, and move food into consumption instead of into storage. It is a program that will remove the threat to the farmer of these overhanging surpluses, a program, also, that will stimulate production when a commodity is scarce and encourage consumption when nature is bountiful. Moreover, it will promote the individual freedom, responsibility, and initiative which distinguish American agriculture. And, by helping our agriculture achieve full parity in the market, it promises our farmers a higher and steadier financial return over the years than any alternative plan.

CONSERVATION

Part of our Nation's precious heritage is its natural resources. It is the common responsibility of Federal, state, and local governments to improve and develop them, always working in the closest harmony and partnership.

All Federal conservation and resource development projects are being reappraised. Sound projects now under way will be continued. New projects in which the Federal Government has a part must be economically sound, with local sharing of cost wherever appropriate and feasible. In the next fiscal year work will be started on twenty-three projects that meet these standards. The Federal Government will continue to construct and operate economically sound flood control, power, irrigation and water supply projects wherever these projects are beyond the capacity of local initiative, public or private, and consistent with the needs of the whole Nation.

Our conservation program will also take into account the important role played by farmers in protecting our soil resources. I recommend enactment of legislation to strengthen agricultural conservation and upstream flood prevention work, and to achieve a better balance with major flood control structures in the down-stream areas.

Recommendations will be made from time to time for the adoption of:

A uniform and consistent water resources policy;

A revised public lands policy; and

A sound program for safeguarding the domestic production of critical and strategic metals and minerals.

In addition we shall continue to protect and improve our national forests, parks, monuments and other natural and historic sites, as well as our fishery and wildlife resources. I hope that pending legislation to improve the conservation and management of publicly-owned grazing lands in national forests will soon be approved by the Congress.

NATIONAL HIGHWAYS

To protect the vital interest of every citizen in a safe and adequate highway system, the Federal Government is continuing its central role in the Federal Aid Highway Program. So that maximum progress can be made to overcome present inadequacies in the Interstate Highway System, we must continue the Federal gasoline tax at two cents per gallon. This will require cancellation of the $\frac{1}{2}$ decrease which otherwise will become effective April 1st, and will maintain revenues so that an expanded highway program can be undertaken.

When the Commission on Intergovernmental Relations completes its study of the present system of financing highway construction, I shall promptly submit it for consideration by the Congress and the governors of the states.

POST OFFICE

It is apparent that the substantial savings already made, and to be made, by the Post Office Department cannot eliminate the postal deficit. I recommend, therefore, that the Congress approve the bill now pending in the House of Representatives providing for the adjustment of certain postal rates. To handle the long term aspects of this, I also recommend that the Congress create a permanent commission to establish fair and reasonable postal rates from time to time in the future.

III. HUMAN PROBLEMS

Along with the protection of freedom and maintenance of a strong and growing economy, this Administration recognizes a third great purpose of government: concern for the human problems of our citizens. In a modern industrial society, banishment of destitution and cushioning the shock of personal disaster on the individual are proper concerns of all levels of government, including the federal government. This is especially true where remedy and prevention alike are beyond the individual's capacity.

LABOR AND WELFARE

Of the many problems in this area, those I shall first discuss are of particular concern to the members of our great labor force, who with their heads, hearts and hands produce so much of the wealth of our country.

Protection against the hazards of temporary unemployment should be extended to some 6S millions of workers, including civilian Federal workers, who now lack this safeguard. Moreover, the Secretary of Labor is making available to the states studies and recommendations in the fields of weekly benefits, periods of protection and extension of coverage. The Economic Report will consider the related matter of minimum wages and their coverage.

The Labor Management Relations Act of 3947 is basically a sound law. However, six years of experience have revealed that in some respects it can be improved. On January 11, I shall forward to the Congress suggestions for changes designed to reinforce the basic objectives of the Act.

Our basic social security program, the Old-Age and Survivors Insurance system, to which individuals contribute during their productive years and receive benefits based on previous earnings, is designed to shield them from destitution. Last year I recommended extension of the social insurance system to include more than 10,000,000 additional persons. I ask that this extension soon be accomplished. This and other major improvements in the insurance system will bring substantial benefit increases and broaden the membership of the insurance system, thus diminishing the need for Federal grants-in-aid for such purposes. A new formula will therefore be proposed, permitting progressive reduction in such grants as the need for them declines.

Federal grant-in-aid welfare programs, now based on widely varying formulas, should be simplified. Concrete proposals on fourteen of them will be suggested to the appropriate Committees.

The program for rehabilitation of the disabled especially needs strengthening. Through special vocational training, this program presently returns each year some 60,000 handicapped individuals to productive work. Far more disabled people can be saved each year from idleness and dependence if this program is gradually increased. My more detailed recommendations on this and the other social insurance problems I have mentioned will be sent to the Congress on January 14th.

HEALTH

I am flatly opposed to the socialization of medicine. The great need for hospital and medical services can best be met by the initiative of private plans. But it is unfortunately a fact that medical costs are rising and already impose severe hardships on many families. The Federal Government can do many helpful things and still carefully avoid the socialization of medicine.

The Federal Government should encourage medical research in its battle with such mortal diseases as cancer and heart ailments, and should continue to help the states in their health and rehabilitation programs. The present Hospital Survey and Construction Act should be broadened in order to assist in the development of adequate facilities for the chronically ill, and to encourage the construction of diagnostic centers, rehabilitation facilities, and nursing homes. The war on disease also needs a better working relationship between Government and private initiative. Private and non-profit hospital and medical insurance plans are already in the field, soundly based on the experience and initiative of the people in their various communities.

A limited Government reinsurance service would permit the private and non-profit insurance companies to offer broader protection to more of the many families which want and should have it. On January 18 I shall forward to the Congress a special message presenting this Administration's health program in its detail.

EDUCATION

Youth—our greatest resource—is being seriously neglected in a vital respect. The nation as a whole is not preparing teachers or building schools fast enough to keep up with the increase in our population.

The preparation of teachers as, indeed, the control and direction of public education policy, is a state and local responsibility. However, the Federal Government should stand ready to assist states which demonstrably cannot provide sufficient school buildings. In order to appraise the needs, I hope that this year a conference on education will be held in each state, culminating in a national conference. From these conferences on education, every level of government—from the Federal Government to each local school board—should gain the information with which to attack this serious problem.

HOUSING

The details of a program to enlarge and improve the opportunities for our people to acquire good homes will be presented to the Congress by special message on January

This program will include:

Modernization of the home mortgage insurance program of the Federal Government;

Redirection of the present system of loans and grants-in-aid to cities for slum clearance and redevelopment;

Extension of the advantages of insured lending to private credit engaged in this task of rehabilitating obsolete neighborhoods;

Insurance of long-term, mortgage loans, with small down payment for low-income families; and, until alternative programs prove more effective,

Continuation of the public housing program adopted in the Housing Act of 1949.

If the individual, the community, the State and federal governments will alike apply themselves, every American family can have a decent home.

VETERANS ADMINISTRATION

The internal reorganization of the Veterans Administration is proceeding with my full approval. When completed, it will afford a single agency whose services, including medical facilities, will be better adapted to the needs of those 20,000,000 veterans to whom this Nation owes so much.

SUFFRAGE

My few remaining recommendations all relate to a basic right of our citizens—that of being represented in the decisions of the government.

I hope that the States will cooperate with the Congress in adopting uniform standards in their voting laws that will make it possible for our citizens in the armed forces overseas to vote.

In the District of Columbia the time is long overdue for granting national suffrage to its citizens and also applying the principle of local self-government to the Nation's Capital. I urge the Congress to move promptly in this direction and also to revise District revenue measures to provide needed public works improvements.

The people of Hawaii are ready for statehood. I renew my request for this legislation in order that Hawaii may elect its State officials and its representatives in Washington along with the rest of the country this fall.

For years our citizens between the ages of 18 and 21 have, in time of peril, been summoned to fight for America. They should participate in the political process that produces this fateful summons. I urge Congress to propose to the States a constitutional amendment permitting citizens to vote when they reach the age of 18.

CONCLUSION

I want to add one final word about the general purport of these many recommendations.

Our government's powers are wisely limited by the Constitution; but quite apart from those limitations, there are things which no government can do or should try to do.

A government can strive, as ours is striving, to maintain an economic system whose doors are open to enterprise and ambition—those personal qualities on which economic growth largely depends. But enterprise and ambition are qualities which no government can supply. Fortunately no American government need concern itself on this score; our people have these qualities in good measure.

A government can sincerely strive for peace, as ours is striving, and ask its people to make sacrifices for the sake of peace. But no government can place peace in the hearts of foreign rulers. It is our duty then to ourselves and to freedom itself to remain strong in all those ways—spiritual, economic, military—that will give us maximum safety against the possibility of aggressive action by others.

No government can inoculate its people against the fatal materialism that plagues our age. Happily, our people, though blessed with more material goods than any people in history, have always reserved their first allegiance to the kingdom of the spirit, which is the true source of that freedom we value above all material things.

But a government can try, as ours tries, to sense the deepest aspirations of the people, and to express them in political action at home and abroad. So long as action and aspiration humbly and earnestly seek favor in the sight of the Almighty, there is no end to America's forward road; there is no obstacle on it she will not surmount in her march toward a lasting peace in a free and prosperous world.

2.3 Dwight D. Eisenhower's Third State of the Union Address

Mr. President, Mr. Speaker, Members of the Congress:

First, I extend cordial greetings to the 84th Congress. We shall have much to do together; I am sure that we shall get it done—and, that we shall do it in harmony and good will.

At the outset, I believe it would be well to remind ourselves of this great fundamental in our national life: our common belief that every human being is divinely endowed with dignity and worth and inalienable rights. This faith, with its corollary—that to grow and flourish people must be free—shapes the interests and aspirations of every American.

From this deep faith have evolved three main purposes of our Federal Government:

First, to maintain justice and freedom among ourselves and to champion them for others so that we may work effectively for enduring peace;

Second, to help keep our economy vigorous and expanding, thus sustaining our international strength and assuring better jobs, better living, better opportunities for every citizen;

And third, to concern ourselves with the human problems of our people so that every American may have the opportunity to lead a healthy, productive and rewarding life.

Foremost among these broad purposes of government is our support of freedom, justice and peace.

It is of the utmost importance, that each of us understand the true nature of the struggle now taking place in the world.

It is not a struggle merely of economic theories, or of forms of government, or of military power. At issue is the true nature of man. Either man is the creature whom the Psalmist described as "a little lower than the angels," crowned with glory and honor, holding "dominion over the works" of his Creator; or man is a soulless, animated machine to be enslaved, used and consumed by the state for its own glorification.

It is, therefore, a struggle which goes to the roots of the human spirit, and its shadow falls across the long sweep of man's destiny. This prize, so precious, so fraught with ultimate meaning, is the true object of the contending forces in the world.

In the past year, there has been progress justifying hope, both for continuing peace and for the ultimate rule of freedom and justice in the world. Free nations are collectively stronger than at any time in recent years.

Just as nations of this Hemisphere, in the historic Caracas and Rio conferences, have closed ranks against imperialistic Communism and strengthened their economic ties, so free nations elsewhere have forged new bonds of unity.

Recent agreements between Turkey and Pakistan have laid a foundation for increased strength in the Middle East. With our understanding support, Egypt and Britain, Yugoslavia and Italy, Britain and Iran have resolved dangerous differences. The security of the Mediterranean has been enhanced by an alliance among Greece, Turkey and Yugoslavia. Agreements in Western Europe have paved the way for unity to replace past divisions which have undermined Europe's economic and military vitality. The defense of the West appears likely at last to include a free, democratic Germany participating as an equal in the councils of NATO.

In Asia and the Pacific, the pending Manila Pact supplements our treaties with Australia, New Zealand, the Philippines,

Korea and Japan and our prospective treaty with the Republic of China. These pacts stand as solemn warning that future military aggression and subversion against the free nations of Asia will meet united response. The Pacific Charter, also adopted at Manila, is a milestone in the development of human freedom and self-government in the Pacific area.

Under the auspices of the United Nations, there is promise of progress in our country's plan for the peaceful use of atomic energy.

Finally, today the world is at peace. It is, to be sure, an secure peace. Yet all humanity finds hope in the simple fact that for an appreciable time there has been no active major battlefield on earth. This same fact inspires us to work all the more effectively with other nations for the well-being, the freedom, the dignity, of every human on earth.

These developments are heartening indeed, and we are hopeful of continuing progress. But sobering problems remain.

The massive military machines and ambitions of the Soviet-Communist bloc still create uneasiness in the world. All of us are aware of the continuing reliance of the Soviet Communists on military force, of the power of their weapons, of their present resistance to realistic armament limitation, and of their continuing effort to dominate or intimidate free nations on their periphery. Their steadily growing power includes an increasing strength in nuclear weapons. This power, combined with the proclaimed intentions of the Communist leaders to communize the world, is the threat confronting us today.

To protect our nations and our peoples from the catastrophe of a nuclear holocaust, free nations must maintain countervailing military power to persuade the Communists of the futility of seeking their ends through aggression. If Communist rulers understand that America's response to aggression will be swift and decisive—that never shall we buy peace at the expense of honor or faith—they will be powerfully deterred from launching a military venture engulfing their own peoples and many others in disaster. This, of course, is merely world stalemate. But in this stalemate each of us may and must exercise his high duty to strive in every honorable way for enduring peace.

The military threat is but one menace to our freedom and security. We must not only deter aggression; we must also frustrate the effort of Communists to gain their goals by subversion. To this end, free nations must maintain and reinforce their cohesion, their internal security, their political and economic vitality, and their faith in freedom. In such a world, America's course is dear: We must tirelessly labor to make the peace more just and durable.

We must strengthen the collective defense under the United Nations Charter and gird ourselves with sufficient military strength and productive capacity to discourage resort to war and protect our nation's vital interests.

We must continue to support and strengthen the United Nations. At this very moment, by vote of the United Nations General Assembly, its Secretary-General is in Communist China on a mission of deepest concern to all Americans: seeking the release of our never-to-be-forgotten American aviators and all other United Nations prisoners wrongfully detained by the Communist regime.

We must also encourage the efforts being made in the United Nations to limit armaments and to harness the atom to peaceful rise.

We must expand international trade and investment and assist friendly nations whose own best efforts are still insufficient to provide the strength essential to the security of the free world.

We must be willing to use the processes of negotiation whenever they will advance the cause of just and secure peace to which the United States and other free nations are dedicated.

In respect to all these matters, we must, through a vigorous information program, keep the peoples of the world truthfully advised of our actions and purposes. This problem has been attacked with new vigor during the past months. I urge that the Congress give its earnest consideration to the great advantages that can accrue to our country through the successful operations of this program.

We must also carry forward our educational exchange program. This sharing of knowledge and experience between our citizens and those of free countries is a powerful factor in the development and maintenance of true partnership among free peoples.

To advance these many efforts, the Congress must act in this session on appropriations, legislation, and treaties. Today I shall mention especially our foreign economic and military programs.

The recent economic progress in many free nations has been most heartening. The productivity of labor and the production of goods and services are increasing in ever-widening areas. There is a growing will to improve the living standards of all men. This progress is important to all our people. It promises us allies who are strong and self-reliant; it promises a growing world market for the products of our mines, our factories, and our farms.

But only through steady effort can we hope to continue this progress. Barriers still impede trade and the flow of capital needed to develop each nation's human and material resources. Wise reduction of these barriers is a long-term objective of our foreign economic policy—a policy of an evolutionary and selective nature, assuring broad benefits to our own and other peoples.

We must gradually reduce certain tariff obstacles to trade. These actions should, of course, be accompanied by a similar lowering of trade barriers by other nations, so that we may move steadily toward greater economic advantage for all. We must further simplify customs administration and procedures. We must facilitate the flow of capital and continue technical assistance, both directly and through the United Nations, to less developed countries to strengthen their independence and raise their living standards. Many another step must be taken in and among the nations of the free world to release forces of private initiative. In our own nation, these forces have brought strength and prosperity; once released, they will generate rising incomes in these other countries with which to buy the products of American industry, labor and agriculture.

On January 10, by special message, I shall submit specific recommendations for carrying forward the legislative phases of our foreign economic policy.

Our many efforts to build a better world include the maintenance of our military strength. This is a vast undertaking. Major national security programs consume two-thirds of the entire Federal budget. Over four million Americans—servicemen and civilians—are on the rolls of the defense establishment. During the past two years, by eliminating duplication and overstaffing, by improved procurement and inventory controls, and by concentrating on the essentials, many billions of dollars have been saved in our defense activities. I should like to mention certain fundamentals underlying this vast program.

First, a realistic limitation of armaments and an enduring, just peace remain our national goals; we maintain powerful military forces because there is no present alternative—forces designed for deterrent and defensive purposes alone but able instantly to strike back with destructive power in response to an attack.

Second, we must stay alert to the fact that undue reliance on one weapon or preparation for only one kind of warfare simply invites an enemy to resort to another. We must, therefore, keep in our armed forces balance and flexibility adequate for our purposes and objectives.

Third, to keep our armed forces abreast of the advances of science, our military planning must be flexible enough to utilize the new weapons and techniques which flow ever more speedily from our research and development programs. The forthcoming military budget therefore emphasizes modern airpower in the Air Force, Navy and Marine Corps and increases the emphasis on new weapons, especially those of rapid and destructive striking power. It assures the maintenance of effective, retaliatory force as the principal deterrent to overt aggression. It accelerates the continental defense program and the build-up of ready military reserve forces. It continues a vigorous program of stockpiling strategic and critical materials and strengthening our mobilization base. The budget also contemplates the strategic concentration of our strength through redeployment of certain forces. It provides for reduction of forces in certain categories and their expansion in others, to fit them to the military realities of our time. These emphases in our defense planning have been made at my personal direction after long and thoughtful study. In my judgment, they will give our nation a defense accurately adjusted to the national need.

Fourth, pending a world agreement on armament limitation, we must continue to improve and expand our supplies of nuclear weapons for our land, naval and air forces, while, at the same time, continuing our encouraging progress in the peaceful use of atomic power.

And fifth, in the administration of these costly programs, we must demand the utmost in efficiency and ingenuity. We must assure our people not only of adequate protection but also of a defense that can be carried forward from year to year until the threat of aggression has disappeared.

To help maintain this kind of armed strength and improve its efficiency, I must urge the enactment of several important measures in this session.

The first concerns the selective service act which expires next June 30th. For the foreseeable future, our standing forces must remain much larger than voluntary methods can sustain. We must, therefore, extend the statutory authority to induct men for two years of military service.

The second kind of measure concerns the rapid turnover of our most experienced servicemen. This process seriously weakens the combat readiness of our armed forces and is exorbitantly expensive. To encourage more trained servicemen to remain in uniform, I shall, on the thirteenth of this month, propose a number of measures to increase the attractions of a military career. These measures will include more adequate medical care for dependents, survivors' benefits, more and better housing, and selective adjustments in military pay and other allowances.

And third—also on January 13—I shall present a program to rebuild and strengthen the civilian components of our armed forces. This is a comprehensive program, designed to make better use of our manpower of military age. Because it will go far in assuring fair and equitable participation in military training and service, it is of particular importance to our combat veterans. In keeping with the historic military policy of our Republic, this program is designed to build and maintain powerful civilian reserves immediately capable of effective military service in an emergency in lieu of maintaining active duty forces in excess of the nation's immediate need.

Maintenance of an effective defense requires continuance of our aggressive attack on subversion at home. In this effort we have, in the past two years, made excellent progress. FBI investigations have been powerfully reinforced by a new Internal Security Division in the Department of Justice; the security activities of the Immigration and Naturalization Service have been revitalized; an improved and strengthened security system is in effect throughout the government; the Department of Justice and the FBI have been armed with effective new legal weapons forged by the 83rd Congress.

We shall continue to ferret out and to destroy Communist subversion.

We shall, in the process, carefully preserve our traditions and the basic rights of our citizens.

Our civil defense program is also a key element in the protection of our country. We are developing cooperative methods with State Governors, Mayors, and voluntary citizen groups, as well as among Federal agencies, in building the civil defense organization. Its significance in time of war is obvious; its swift assistance in disaster areas last year proved its importance in time of peace.

An industry capable of rapid expansion and essential materials and facilities swiftly available in time of emergency are indispensable to our defense. I urge, therefore, a two-year extension of the Defense Production Act and Title II of the First War Powers Act of 1941. These are cornerstones of our program for the development and maintenance of an adequate mobilization base. At this point, I should like to make this additional observation. Our quest for peace and freedom necessarily presumes that we who hold positions of public trust must rise above self and section—that we must subordinate to the general good our partisan, our personal pride and prejudice. Tirelessly, with united purpose, we must fortify the material and spiritual foundations of this land of freedom and of free nations throughout the world. As never before, there is need for unhesitating cooperation among the branches of our government.

At this time the executive and legislative branches are under the management of different political parties. This fact places both parties on trial before the American people.

In less perilous days of the past, division of governmental responsibility among our great parties has produced a paralyzing indecision. We must not let this happen in our time. We must avoid a paralysis of the will for peace and international security.

In the traditionally bipartisan areas—military security and foreign relations—I can report to you that I have already, with the leaders of this Congress, expressed assurances of unreserved cooperation. Yet, the strength of our country requires more than mere maintenance of military strength and success in foreign affairs; these vital matters are in turn dependent upon concerted and vigorous action in a number of supporting programs. I say, therefore, to the 84th Congress:

In all areas basic to the strength of America, there will be—to the extent I can insure them—cooperative, constructive relations between the Executive and Legislative Branches of this government. Let the general good be our yardstick on every great issue of our time.

Our efforts to defend our freedom and to secure a just peace are, of course, inseparable from the second great purpose of our government: to help maintain a strong, growing economy—an economy vigorous and free, in which there are ever-increasing opportunities, just rewards for effort, and a stable prosperity that is widely shared.

In the past two years, many important governmental Actions helped our economy adjust to conditions of peace; these and other actions created a climate for renewed economic growth. Controls were removed from wages, prices and materials. Tax revisions encouraged increased private spending and employment. Federal expenditures were sharply reduced, making possible a record tax cut. These actions, together with flexible monetary and debt management policies, helped to halt inflation and stabilize the value of the dollar. A program of cooperation and partnership in resource development was begun. Social security and unemployment insurance laws were broadened and strengthened. New laws started the long process of balancing farm production with farm markets. Expanded shipbuilding and stockpiling programs strengthened key sectors of the economy, while improving our mobilization base. A comprehensive new housing law brought impressive progress in an area fundamental to our economic strength and closed loopholes in the old laws permitting dishonest manipulation. Many of these programs are just beginning to exert their main stimulating effect upon the economy generally and upon specific communities and industries throughout the country.

The past year—1954—was one of the most prosperous years in our history. Business activity now surges with new strength. Production is rising. Employment is high. Toward the end of last year average weekly wages in manufacturing were higher than ever before. Personal income after taxes is at a record level. So is consumer spending. Construction activity is reaching new peaks. Export demand for our goods is strong. State and local government expenditures on public works are rising. Savings are high, and credit is readily available.

So, today, the transition to a peacetime economy is largely behind us. The economic outlook is good.

The many promising factors I have mentioned do not guarantee sustained economic expansion; however, they do give us a strong position from which to carry forward our economic growth. If we as a people act wisely, within ten years our annual national output can rise from its present level of about $360 billion to $500 billion, measured in dollars of stable buying power.

My Budget Message on January 17, the Economic Report on the 20th of this month, and several special messages will set forth in detail major programs to foster the growth of our economy and to protect the integrity of the people's money. Today I shall discuss these programs only in general terms.

Government efficiency and economy remain essential to steady progress toward a balanced budget. More than ten billion dollars were cut from the spending program proposed in the budget of January 9, 1953. Expenditures of that year were six and a half billion below those of the previous year. In the current fiscal year, government spending will be nearly four and a half billion dollars less than in the fiscal year which ended last June 30. New spending authority has been held below expenditures, reducing government obligations accumulated over the years.

Last year we had a large tax cut and, for the first time in seventy-five years a basic revision of Federal tax laws. It is now clear that defense and other essential government costs must remain at a level precluding further tax reductions this year. Although excise and corporation income taxes must, therefore, be continued at their present rates, further tax cuts will be possible when justified by lower expenditures and by revenue increases arising from the nation's economic growth. I am hopeful that such reductions can be made next year.

At the foundation of our economic growth are the raw materials and energy produced from our minerals and fuels, lands and forests, and water resources. With respect to them, I believe that the nation must adhere to three fundamental policies: first, to develop, wisely use and conserve basic resources from generation to generation; second, to follow the historic pattern of developing these resources primarily by private citizens under fair provisions of law, including restraints for proper conservation; and third, to treat resource development as a partnership undertaking—a partnership in which the participation of private citizens and State and local governments is as necessary as Federal participation.

This policy of partnership and cooperation is producing good results, most immediately noticeable in respect to water resources. First, it has encouraged local public bodies and private citizens to plan their own power sources. Increasing numbers of applications to the Federal Power Commission to conduct surveys and prepare plans for power development, notably in the Columbia River Basin, are evidence of local response.

Second, the Federal Government and local and private organizations have been encouraged to coordinate their developments. This is important because Federal hydroelectric developments supply but a small fraction of the nation's power needs. Such partnership projects as Priest Rapids in Washington, the Coosa River development in Alabama, and Markham Ferry in Oklahoma already have the approval of the Congress. This year justifiable projects of a similar nature will again have Administration support.

Third, the Federal Government must shoulder its own partnership obligations by undertaking projects of such complexity and size that their success requires Federal development. In keeping with this principle, I again urge the Congress to approve the development of the Upper Colorado River Basin to conserve and assure better use of precious water essential to the future of the West.

In addition, the 1956 budget will recommend appropriations to start six new reclamation and more than thirty new Corps of Engineers projects of varying size. Going projects and investigations of potential new resource developments will be continued.

Although this partnership approach is producing encouraging results, its full success requires a nation-wide comprehensive water resources policy firmly based in law. Such a policy is under preparation and when completed will be submitted to the Congress.

In the interest of their proper conservation, development and use, continued vigilance will be maintained over our fisheries, wildlife resources, the national parks and forests, and the public lands; and we shall continue to encourage an orderly development of the nation's mineral resources.

A modern, efficient highway system is essential to meet the needs of our growing population, our expanding economy, and our national security. We are accelerating our highway improvement program as rapidly as possible under existing State and Federal laws and authorizations. However, this effort will not in itself assure our people of an adequate highway system. On my recommendation, this problem has been carefully considered by the Conference of State Governors and by a special Advisory Committee on a National Highway Program, composed of leading private citizens. I have received the recommendations of the Governors' Conference and will shortly receive the views of the special Advisory Committee. Aided by their findings, I shall submit on January 27th detailed recommendations which will meet our most pressing national highway needs.

In further recognition of the importance of transportation to our economic strength and security, the Administration, through a Cabinet committee, is thoroughly examining existing Federal transportation policies to determine their effect on the adequacy of transportation services. This is the first such comprehensive review directly undertaken by the Executive Branch of the government in modern times. We are not only examining major problems facing the various modes of transport; we are also studying closely the inter-relationships of civilian and government requirements for transportation. Legislation will be recommended to correct policy deficiencies which we may find.

The nation's public works activities are tremendous in scope. It is expected that more than $ 12 billion will be expended in 1955 for the development of land, water and other resources; control of floods, and navigation and harbor improvements; construction of roads, schools, and municipal water supplies, and disposal of domestic and industrial wastes. Many of the Federal, State and local agencies responsible for this work are, in their separate capacities, highly efficient. But public works activities are closely inter-related and have a substantial influence on the growth of the country. Moreover, in times of threatening economic contraction, they may become a valuable sustaining force. To these ends, efficient planning and execution of the nation's public works require both the coordination of Federal activities and effective cooperation with State and local governments.

The Council of Economic Advisers, through its public works planning section, has made important advances during the past year in effecting this coordination and cooperation. In view of the success of these initial efforts, and to give more emphasis and continuity to this essential coordination, I shall request the Congress to appropriate funds for the support of an Office of Coordinator of Public Works in the Executive Office of the President.

A most significant element in our growing economy is an agriculture that is stable, prosperous and free. The problems of our agriculture have evolved over many years and cannot be solved overnight; nevertheless, governmental actions last year hold great promise of fostering a better balance between production and markets and, consequently, a better and more stable income for our farmers.

Through vigorous administration and through new authority provided by the 83rd Congress, surplus farm products are now moving into consumption. From February 1953 through November 1954, the rate of increase of government-held surpluses has been reduced by our moving into use more than 2.3 billion dollars' worth of government-owned farm commodities; this amount is equal to more than seven percent of a year's production of all our farms and ranches. Domestic consumption remains high, and farm exports will be higher than last year. As a result of the flexibility provided by the Agricultural Act of 1954, we can move toward less restrictive acreage controls.

Thus, farm production is gradually adjusting to markets, markets are being expanded, and stocks are moving into use. We can now look forward to an easing of the influences depressing farm prices, to reduced government expenditures for purchase of surplus products, and to less Federal intrusion into the lives and plans of our farm people. Agricultural programs have been redirected toward better balance, greater stability and sustained prosperity. We are headed in the right direction. I urgently recommend to the Congress that we continue resolutely on this road.

Greater attention must be directed to the needs of low-income farm families. Twenty-eight per cent of our farm-operator families have net cash incomes of less than $1,000 per year. Last year, at my request, careful studies were made of the problems of these farm people. I shall later submit recommendations designed to assure the steady alleviation of their most pressing concerns.

Because drought also remains a serious agricultural problem, I shall recommend legislation to strengthen Federal disaster assistance programs. This legislation will prescribe an improved appraisal of need, better adjustment of the various programs to local conditions, and a more equitable sharing of costs between the States and the Federal Government.

The prosperity of our small business enterprises is an indispensable element in the maintenance of our economic strength. Creation of the Small Business Administration and recently enacted tax laws facilitating small business expansion are but two of many important steps we have taken to encourage our smaller enterprises. I recommend that the Congress extend the Small Business Act of 1953 which is due to expire next June.

We come now to the third great purpose of our government-its concern for the health, productivity and well-being of all our people.

Every citizen wants to give full expression to his God-given talents and abilities and to have the recognition and respect accorded under our religious and political traditions. Americans also want a good material standard of living—not simply to accumulate possessions, but to fulfill a legitimate aspiration for an environment in which their families may live meaningful and happy lives. Our people are committed, therefore, to the creation and preservation of opportunity for every citizen to lead a more rewarding life. They are equally committed to the alleviation of misfortune and distress among their fellow citizens.

The aspirations of most of our people can best be fulfilled through their own enterprise and initiative, without government interference. This Administration, therefore, follows two simple rules: first, the Federal Government should perform an essential task only when it cannot otherwise be adequately performed; and second, in performing that task, our government must not impair the self-respect, freedom and incentive of the individual. So long as these two rules are observed, the government can fully meet its obligation without creating a dependent population or a domineering bureaucracy.

During the past two years, notable advances were made in these functions of government. Protection of old-age and survivors' insurance was extended to an additional ten million of our people, and the benefits were substantially increased. Legislation was enacted to provide unemployment insurance protection to some four million additional Americans. Stabilization of living costs and the halting of inflation protected the value of pensions and savings. A broad program now helps to bring good homes within the reach of the great majority of our people. With the States, we are providing rehabilitation facilities and more clinics, hospitals, and nursing homes for patients with chronic illnesses. Also with the States, we have begun a great and fruitful expansion in the restoration of disabled persons to employment and useful lives. In the areas of Federal responsibility, we have made historic progress in eliminating from among our people demeaning practices based on race or color.

All of us may be proud of these achievements during the past two years. Yet essential Federal tasks remain to be done.

As part of our efforts to provide decent, safe and sanitary housing for low-income families, we must carry forward the housing program authorized during the 83rd Congress. We must also authorize contracts for a firm program of 35,000 additional public housing units in each of the next two fiscal years. This program will meet the most pressing obligations of the Federal Government into the 1958 fiscal year for planning and building public housing. By that time the private building industry, aided by the Housing Act of 1954, will have had the opportunity to assume its full role in providing adequate housing for our low income families.

The health of our people is one of our most precious assets. Preventable sickness should be prevented; knowledge available to combat disease and disability should be fully used. Otherwise, we as a people are guilty not only of neglect of human suffering but also of wasting our national strength.

Constant advances in medical care are not available to enough of our citizens. Clearly our nation must do more to reduce the impact of accident and disease. Two fundamental problems confront us: first, high and ever-rising costs of health services; second, serious gaps and shortages in these services.

By special message on January 24, I shall propose a coordinated program to strengthen and improve existing health services. This program will continue to reject socialized medicine. It will emphasize individual and local responsibility. Under it the Federal Government will neither dominate nor direct, but serve as a helpful partner. Within this framework, the program can be broad in scope.

My recommendations will include a Federal health reinsurance service to encourage the development of more and better voluntary health insurance coverage by private organizations. I shall also recommend measures to improve the medical care of that group of our citizens who, because of need, receive Federal-State public assistance. These two proposals will help more of our people to meet the costs of health services. To reduce the gaps in these services, I shall propose:

New measures to facilitate construction of needed health facilities and help reduce shortages of trained health personnel; Vigorous steps to combat the misery and national loss involved in mental illness; Improved services for crippled children and for maternal and child health;

Better consumer protection under our existing pure food and drug laws; and, finally, Strengthened programs to combat the increasingly serious pollution of our rivers and streams and the growing problem of air pollution.

These measures together constitute a comprehensive program holding rich promise for better health for all of our people.

Last year's expansion of social security coverage and our new program of improved medical care for public assistance recipients together suggest modification of the formula for Federal sharing in old age assistance payments. I recommend modification of the formula where such payments will, in the future, supplement benefits received under the old age and survivors insurance system.

It is the inalienable right of every person, from childhood on, to have access to knowledge. In our form of society, this right of the individual takes on a special meaning, for the education of all our citizens is imperative to the maintenance and invigoration of America's free institutions.

Today, we face grave educational problems. Effective and up-to-date analyses of these problems and their solutions are being carried forward through the individual State conferences and the White House Conference to be completed this year.

However, such factors as population growth, additional responsibilities of schools, and increased and longer school attendance have produced an unprecedented classroom shortage. This shortage is of immediate concern to all of our people. Positive, affirmative action must be taken now.

Without impairing in any way the responsibilities of our States, localities, communities, or families, the Federal government can and should serve as an effective-catalyst in dealing with this problem. I shall forward a special message to the Congress on February 15, presenting an affirmative program dealing with this shortage.

To help the States do a better and more timely job, we must strengthen their resources for preventing and dealing with juvenile delinquency. I shall propose Federal legislation to assist the States to promote concerted action in dealing with this nationwide problem. I shall carry forward the vigorous efforts of the Administration to improve the international control of the traffic in narcotics and, in cooperation with State and local agencies, to combat narcotic addiction in our country.

I should like to speak now of additional matters of importance to all our people and especially to our wage earners.

During the past year certain industrial changes and the readjustment of the economy to conditions of peace brought unemployment and other difficulties to various localities and industries. These problems are engaging our most earnest attention. But for the overwhelming majority of our working people, the past year has meant good jobs. Moreover, the earnings and savings of our wage earners are no longer depreciating in value. Because of cooperative relations between labor and management, fewer working days were lost through strikes in 1954 than in any year in the past decade.

The outlook for our wage earners can be made still more promising by several legislative actions.

First, in the past five years we have had economic growth which will support an increase in the Federal minimum wage. In the light of present economic conditions, I recommend its increase to ninety cents an hour. I also recommend that many others, at present excluded, be given the protection of a minimum wage.

Second, I renew my recommendation of last year for amendment of the Labor Management Relations Act of 1947 to further the basic objectives of this statute. I especially call to the attention of the Congress amendments dealing with the right of economic strikers to vote in representation elections and the need for equalizing the obligation under the Act to file disclaimers of Communist affiliation.

Third, the Administration will propose other important measures including occupational safety, workmen's compensation for longshoremen and harbor workers, and the "Eight Hour Laws" applicable to Federal contractors. Legislation will also be proposed respecting nonoccupational disability insurance and unemployment compensation in the District of Columbia.

In considering human needs, the Federal Government must take special responsibility for citizens in its direct employ. On January 11 I shall propose a pay adjustment plan for civilian employees outside the Postal Field Service to correct inequities and increase individual pay rates. I shall also recommend voluntary health insurance on a contributory basis for Federal employees and their dependents. In keeping with the Group Life Insurance Act passed in the 83rd Congress, this protection should be provided on the group insurance principle and purchased from private facilities. Also on January 11 I shall recommend a modern pay plan, including pay increases, for postal field employees. As part of this program, and to carry forward our progress toward elimination of the large annual postal deficit. I shall renew my request for an increase in postal rates. Again I urge that in the future the fixing of rates be delegated to an impartial, independent body.

More adequate training programs to equip career employees of the government to render improved public service will be recommended, as will improvements in the laws affecting employees serving on foreign assignments.

Needed improvements in survivor, disability, and retirement benefits for Federal civilian and military personnel have been extensively considered by the Committee on Retirement Policy for Federal personnel. The Committee's proposals would strengthen and improve benefits for our career people in government, and I endorse their broad objectives. Full contributory coverage under old-age and survivors' insurance should be made available to all Federal personnel, just as in private industry. For career military personnel, the protection of the old-age and survivors' insurance system would be an important and long-needed addition, especially to their present unequal and inadequate survivorship protection. The military retirement pay system should remain separate and unchanged. Certain adjustments in the present civilian personnel retirement systems will be needed to reflect the additional protection of old-age and survivors' insurance. However, these systems also are a basic part of a total compensation and should be separately and independently retained.

I also urge the Congress to approve a long overdue increase in the salaries of Members of the Congress and of the Federal judiciary to a level commensurate with their heavy responsibilities.

Our concern for the individual in our country requires that we consider several additional problems.

We must continue our program to help our Indian citizens improve their lot and make their full contribution to national life. Two years ago I advised the Congress of injustices under existing immigration laws. Through humane administration, the Department of Justice is doing what it legally can to alleviate hardships. Clearance of aliens before arrival has been initiated, and except for criminal offenders, the imprisonment of aliens awaiting admission or deportation has been stopped. Certain provisions of law, however, have the effect of compelling action in respect to aliens which are inequitable in some instances and discriminatory in others. These provisions should be corrected in this session of the Congress.

As the complex problems of Alaska are resolved, that Territory should expect to achieve statehood. In the meantime, there is no justification for deferring the admission to statehood of Hawaii. I again urge approval of this measure.

We have three splendid opportunities to demonstrate the strength of our belief in the right of suffrage. First, I again urge that a Constitutional amendment be submitted to the States to reduce the voting age for Federal elections. Second, I renew my request that the principle of self-government be extended and the right of suffrage granted to the citizens of the District of Columbia. Third, I again recommend that we work with the States to preserve the voting fights of citizens in the nation's service overseas.

In our determination to keep faith with those who in the past have met the highest call of citizenship, we now have under study the system of benefits for veterans and for surviving dependents of deceased veterans and servicemen. Studies will be undertaken to determine the need for measures to ease the readjustment to civilian life of men required to enter the armed forces for two years of service.

In the advancement of the various activities which will make our civilization endure and flourish, the Federal Government should do more to give official recognition to the importance of the arts and other cultural activities. I shall recommend the establishment of a Federal Advisory Commission on the Arts within the Department of Health, Education and Welfare, to advise the Federal Government on ways to encourage artistic endeavor and appreciation. I shall also propose that awards of merit be established whereby we can honor our fellow citizens who make great contribution to the advancement of our civilization.

Every citizen rightly expects efficient and economical administration of these many government programs I have outlined today. I strongly recommend extension of the Reorganization Act and the law establishing the Commission on Intergovernmental Relations, both of which expire this spring. Thus the Congress will assure continuation of the excellent progress recently made in improving government organization and administration. In this connection we are looking forward with great interest to the reports which will soon be going to the Congress from the Commission on Organization of the Executive Branch of the Government. I am sure that these studies, made under the chairmanship of former President Herbert Hoover with the assistance of more than two hundred distinguished citizens, will be of great value in paving the way toward more efficiency and economy in the government.

And now, I return to the point at which I began—the faith of our people. The many programs here summarized are, I believe, in full keeping with their needs, interests and aspirations. The obligations upon us are clear:

To labor earnestly, patiently, prayerfully, for peace, for freedom, for justice, throughout the world; To keep our economy vigorous and free, that our people may lead fuller, happier lives;

To advance, not merely by our words but by our acts, the determination of our government that every citizen shall have opportunity to develop to his fullest capacity. As we do these things, before us is a future filled with opportunity and hope. That future will be ours if in our time we keep alive the patience, the courage, the confidence in tomorrow, the deep faith, of the millions who, in years past, made and preserved us this nation.

A decade ago, in the death and desolation of European battlefields, I saw the courage and resolution, I felt the inspiration, of American youth. In these young men I felt America's buoyant confidence and irresistible will-to-do. In them I saw, too, a devout America, humble before God.

And so, I know with all my heart—and I deeply believe that all Americans know—that, despite the anxieties of this divided world, our faith, and the cause in which we all believe, will surely prevail.

2.4   Dwight D. Eisenhower's Fourth State of the Union Address

To the Congress of the United States:

The opening of this new year must arouse in us all grateful thanks to a kind Providence whose protection has been ever present and whose bounty has been manifold and abundant. The State of the Union today demonstrates what can be accomplished under God by a free people; by their vision, their understanding of national problems, their initiative, their self-reliance, their capacity for work—and by their willingness to sacrifice whenever sacrifice is needed.

In the past three years, responding to what our people want their Government to do, the Congress and the Executive have done much in building a stronger, better America. There has been broad progress in fostering the energies of our people, in providing greater opportunity for the satisfaction of their need, s, and in fulfilling their demands for the strength and security of the Republic.

Our country is at peace. Our security posture commands respect. A spiritual vigor marks our national life. Our economy, approaching the 400 billion dollar mark, is at an unparalleled level of prosperity. The national income is more widely and fairly distributed than ever before. The number of Americans at work has reached an all-time high. As a people, we are achieving ever higher standards of living—earning more, producing more, consuming more, building more and investing more than ever before.

Virtually all sectors of our society are sharing in these good times. Our farm families, if we act wisely, imaginatively and promptly to strengthen our present farm programs, can also look forward to sharing equitably in the prosperity they have helped to create.

War in Korea ended two and a half years ago. The collective security system has been powerfully strengthened. Our defenses have been reinforced at sharply reduced costs. Programs to expand world trade and to harness the atom for the betterment of mankind have been carried forward. Our economy has been freed from governmental wage and price controls. Inflation has been halted; the cost of living stabilized.

Government spending has been cut by more than ten billion dollars. Nearly three hundred thousand positions have been eliminated from the Federal payroll. Taxes have been substantially reduced. A balanced budget is in prospect. Social security has been extended to ten million more Americans and unemployment insurance to four million more. Unprecedented advances in civil rights have been made. The long-standing and deep-seated problems of agriculture have been forthrightly attacked.

This record of progress has been accomplished with a self imposed caution against unnecessary and unwise interference in the private affairs of our people, of their communities and of the several States.

If we of the Executive and Legislative Branches, keeping this caution ever in mind, address ourselves to the business of the year before us—and to the unfinished business of last year—with resolution, the outlook is bright with promise.

Many measures of great national importance recommended last year to the Congress still demand immediate attention legislation for school and highway construction; health and immigration legislation; water resources legislation; legislation to complete the implementation of our foreign economic policy; such labor legislation as amendments of the Labor-Management Relations Act, extension of the Fair Labor Standards Act to additional groups not now covered, and occupational safety legislation; and legislation for construction of an atomic-powered exhibit vessel.

Many new items of business likewise require our attention-measures that will further promote the release of the energies of our people; that will broaden opportunity for all of them; that will advance the Republic in its leadership toward a just peace; measures, in short, that are essential to the building of an everstronger, ever-better America.

Every political and economic guide supports a valid confidence that wise effort will be rewarded by an even more plentiful harvest of human benefit than we now enjoy. Our resources are too many, our principles too dynamic, our purposes too worthy and the issues at stake too immense for us to entertain doubt or fear. But our responsibilities require that we approach this year's business with a sober humility.

A heedless pride in our present strength and position would blind us to the facts of the past, to the pitfalls of the future. We must walk ever in the knowledge that we are enriched by a heritage earned in the labor and sacrifice of our forebears; that, for our children's children, we are trustees of a great Republic and a time-tested political system; that we prosper as a cooperating member of the family of nations.

In this light the Administration has continued work on its program for the Republic, begun three years ago. Because the. vast spread of national and human interests is involved within it, I shall not in this Message attempt its detailed delineation. Instead, from time to time during this Session, there will be submitted to the Congress specific recommendations within specific fields. In the comprehensive survey required for their preparation, the Administration is guided by enduring objectives. The first is:

THE DISCHARGE OF OUR WORLD RESPONSIBILITY

Our world policy and our actions are dedicated to the achievement of peace with justice for all nations.

With this purpose, we move in a wide variety of ways and through many agencies to remove the pall of fear; to strengthen the ties with our partners and to improve the cooperative cohesion of the free world; to reduce the burden of armaments, and to stimulate and inspire action among all nations for a world of justice and prosperity and peace. These national objectives are fully supported by both our political parties.

In the past year, our search for a more stable and just peace has taken varied forms. Among the most important were the two Conferences at Geneva, in July and in the fall of last year. We explored the possibilities of agreement on critical issues that jeopardize the peace.

The July meeting of Heads of Government held out promise to the world of moderation in the bitterness, of word and action, which tends to generate conflict and war. All were in agreement that a nuclear war would be an intolerable disaster which must not be permitted to occur. But in October, when the Foreign Ministers met again, the results demonstrated conclusively that the Soviet leaders are not yet willing to create the indispensable conditions for a secure and lasting peace.

Nevertheless, it is clear that the conflict between international communism and freedom has taken on a new complexion.

We know the Communist leaders have often practiced the tactics of retreat and zigzag. We know that Soviet and Chinese communism still poses a serious threat to the free world. And in the Middle East recent Soviet moves are hardly compatible with the reduction of international tension.

Yet Communist tactics against the free nations have shifted in emphasis from reliance on violence and the threat of violence to reliance on division, enticement and duplicity. We must be well prepared to meet the current tactics which pose a dangerous though less obvious threat. At the same time, our policy must be dynamic as well as flexible, designed primarily to forward the achievement of our own objectives rather than to meet each shift and change on the Communist front. We must act in the firm assurance that the fruits of freedom are more attractive and desirable to mankind in the pursuit of happiness than the record of Communism.

In the face of Communist military power, we must, of course, continue to maintain an effective system of collective security. This involves two things—a system which gives clear warning that armed aggression will be met by joint action of the free nations, and deterrent military power to make that warning effective. Moreover, the awesome power of the atom must be made to serve as a guardian of the free community and of the peace.

In the last year, the free world has seen major gains for the system of collective security: the accession to the North Atlantic Treaty Organization and Western European Union of the sovereign Federal German Republic; the developing cooperation under the Southeast Asia Collective Defense Treaty; and the formation in the Middle East of the Baghdad Pact among Turkey, Iraq, Iran, Pakistan and the United Kingdom. In our own hemisphere, the inter-American system has continued to show its vitality in maintaining peace and a common approach to world problems. We now have security pacts with more than 40 other nations.

In the pursuit of our national purposes, we have been steadfast in our support of the United Nations, now entering its second decade with a wider membership and ever-increasing influence and usefulness. In the release of our fifteen fliers from Communist China, an essential prelude was the world opinion mobilized by the General Assembly, which condemned their imprisonment and demanded their liberation. The successful Atomic Energy Conference held in Geneva under United Nations auspices and our Atoms for Peace program have been practical steps toward the world-wide use of this new energy source. Our sponsorship of such use has benefited our relations with other countries. Active negotiations are now in progress to create an International Agency to foster peaceful uses of atomic energy.

During the past year the crucial problem of disarmament has moved to the forefront of practical political endeavor. At Geneva, I declared the readiness of the United States to exchange blueprints of the military establishments of our nation and the USSR, to be confirmed by reciprocal aerial reconnaissance. By this means, I felt mutual suspicions could be allayed and an atmosphere developed in which negotiations looking toward limitation of arms would have improved chances of success.

In the United Nations Subcommittee on Disarmament last fall, this proposal was explored and the United States also declared itself willing to include reciprocal ground inspection of key points. By the overwhelming vote of 56 to 7, the United Nations on December 16 endorsed these proposals and gave them a top priority. Thereby, the issue is placed squarely before the bar of world opinion. We shall persevere in seeking a general reduction of armaments under effective inspection and control which are essential safeguards to ensure reciprocity and protect the security of all.

In the coming year much remains to be done.

While maintaining our military deterrent, we must intensify our efforts to achieve a just peace. In Asia we shall continue to give help to nations struggling to maintain their freedom against the threat of Communist coercion or subversion. In Europe we shall endeavor to increase not only the military strength of the North Atlantic Alliance but also its political cohesion and unity of purpose. We shall give such assistance as is feasible to the recently renewed effort of Western European nations to achieve a greater measure of integration, such as in the field of peaceful uses of atomic energy.

In the Near East we shall spare no effort in seeking to promote a fair solution of the tragic dispute between the Arab States and Israel, all of whom we want as our friends. The United States is ready to do its part to assure enduring peace in that area. We hope that both sides will make the contributions necessary to achieve that purpose. In Latin America, we shall continue to cooperate vigorously in trade and other measures designed to assist economic progress in the area.

Strong economic ties are an essential element in our free world partnership. Increasing trade and investment help all of us prosper together. Gratifying progress has been made in this direction, most recently by the three-year extension of our trade agreements legislation.

I most earnestly request that the Congress approve our membership in the Organization for Trade Cooperation, which would assist the carrying out of the General Agreement on Tariffs and Trade to which we have been a party since 1948.

Our membership in the OTC will provide the most effective and expeditious means for removing discriminations and restrictions against American exports and in making our trade agreements truly reciprocal. United States membership in the Organization will evidence our continuing desire to cooperate in promoting an expanded trade among the free nations. Thus the Organization, as proposed, is admirably suited to our own interests and to those of like-minded nations in working for steady expansion of trade and closer economic cooperation. Being strictly an administrative entity, the Organization for Trade Cooperation cannot, of course, alter the control by Congress of the tariff, import, and customs policies of the United States.

We need to encourage investment overseas by avoiding unfair tax duplications, and to foster foreign trade by further simplification and improvement of our customs legislation.

We must sustain and fortify our Mutual Security Program. Because the conditions of poverty and unrest in less developed areas make their people a special target of international communism, there is a need to help them achieve the economic growth and stability necessary to preserve their independence against communist threats and enticements.

In order that our friends may better achieve the greater strength that is our common goal, they need assurance of continuity in economic assistance for development projects and programs which we approve and which require a period of years for planning and completion. Accordingly, I ask Congress to grant limited authority to make longer-term commitments for assistance to such projects, to be fulfilled from appropriations to be made in future fiscal years.

These various steps will powerfully strengthen the economic foundation of our foreign policy. Together with constructive action abroad, they will maintain the present momentum toward general economic progress and vitality of the free world.

In all things, change is the inexorable law of life. In much of the world the ferment of change is working strongly; but grave injustices are still uncorrected. We must not, by any sanction of ours, help to perpetuate these wrongs. I have particularly in mind the oppressive division of the German people, the bondage of millions elsewhere, and the exclusion of Japan from United Nations membership.

We shall keep these injustices in the forefront of human consciousness and seek to maintain the pressure of world opinion to fight these vast wrongs in the interest both of justice and secure peace.

Injustice thrives on ignorance. Because an understanding of the truth about America is one of our most powerful forces, I am recommending a substantial increase in budgetary support of the United States Information Agency.

The sum of our international effort should be this: the waging of peace, with as much resourcefulness, with as great a sense of dedication and urgency, as we have ever mustered in defense of our country in time of war. In this effort, our weapon is not force. Our weapons are the principles and ideas embodied in our historic traditions, applied with the same vigor that in the past made America a living promise of freedom for all mankind.

To accomplish these vital tasks, all of us should be concerned with the strength, effectiveness and morale .of our State Department and our Foreign Service.

Another guide in the preparation of the Administration's program is:

THE CONSTANT IMPROVEMENT OF OUR NATIONAL SECURITY

Because peace is the keystone of our national policy, our defense program emphasizes an effective flexible type of power calculated to deter or repulse any aggression and to preserve the peace. Short of war, we have never had military strength better adapted to our needs with improved readiness for emergency use. The maintenance of this strong military capability for the indefinite future will continue to call for a large share of our national budget. Our military programs must meet the needs of today. To build less would expose the nation to aggression. To build excessively, under the influence of fear, could defeat our purposes and impair or destroy the very freedom and economic system our military defenses are designed to protect.

We have improved the effectiveness and combat readiness of our forces by developing and making operational new weapons and by integrating the latest scientific developments, including new atomic weapons, into our military plans. We continue to push the production of the most modern military aircraft. The development of long-range missiles has been on an accelerated basis for some time. We are moving as rapidly as practicable toward nuclear-powered aircraft and ships. Combat capability, especially in terms of firepower, has been substantially increased. We have made the adjustments in personnel permitted by the cessation of the Korean War, the buildup of our allies and the introduction of new weapons. The services are all planning realistically on a long-term basis.

To strengthen our continental defenses the United States and Canada, in the closest cooperation, have substantially augmented early warning networks. Great progress is being made in extending surveillance of the Arctic, the Atlantic and the Pacific approaches to North America.

In the last analysis our real strength lies in the caliber of the men and women in our Armed Forces, active and Reserve. Much has been done to attract and hold capable military personnel, but more needs to be done. This year, I renew my request of last year for legislation to provide proper medical care for military dependents and a more equitable survivors' benefit program. The Administration will prepare additional recommendations designed to achieve the same objectives, including career incentives for medical and dental officers and nurses, and increases in the proportion of regular officers.

Closely related to the mission of the Defense Department is the task of the Federal Civil Defense Administration. A particular point of relationship arises from the fact that the key to civil defense is the expanded continental defense program, including the distant early warning system. Our Federal civil defense authorities have made progress in their program, and now comprehensive studies are being conducted jointly by the Federal Civil Defense Administration, the States, and critical target cities to determine the best procedures that can be adopted in case of an atomic attack. We must strengthen Federal assistance to the States and cities in devising the most effective common defense.

We have a broad and diversified mobilization base. We have the facilities, materials, skills and knowledge rapidly to expand the production of things we need for our defense whenever they are required. But mobilization base requirements change with changing technology and strategy. We must maintain flexibility to meet new requirements. I am requesting, therefore, that the Congress once again extend the Defense Production Act.

Of great importance to our nation's security is a continuing alertness to internal subversive activity within or without our government. This Administration will not relax its efforts to deal forthrightly and vigorously in protection of this government and its citizens against subversion, at the same time fully protecting the constitutional rights of all citizens.

A third objective of the Administration is:

FISCAL INTEGRITY

A public office is, indeed, a public trust. None of its aspects is more demanding than the proper management of the public finances. I refer now not only to the indispensable virtues of plain honesty and trustworthiness but also to the prudent, effective and conscientious use of tax money. I refer also to the attitude of mind that makes efficient and economical service to the people a watchword in our government.

Over the long term, a balanced budget is a sure index to thrifty management—in a home, in a business or in the Federal Government. When achievement of a balanced budget is for long put off in a business or home, bankruptcy is the result. But in similar circumstances a government resorts to inflation of the money supply. This inevitably results in depreciation of the value of the money, and an increase in the cost of living. Every investment in personal security is threatened by this process of inflation, and the real values of the people's savings, whether in the form of insurance, bonds, pension and retirement funds or savings accounts are thereby shriveled.

We have made long strides these past three years in bringing our Federal finances under control. The deficit for fiscal year 1953 was almost 9-1/2 billion dollars. Larger deficits seemed certain—deficits which would have depreciated the value of the dollar and pushed the cost of living still higher. But government waste and extravagance were searched out. Nonessential activities were dropped. Government expenses were carefully scrutinized. Total spending was cut by 14 billion dollars below the amount planned by the previous Administration for the fiscal year 1954.

This made possible—and it was appropriate in the existing circumstances of transition to a peacetime economy—the largest tax cut in any year in our history. Almost 7-S billion dollars were released and every taxpayer in the country benefited. Almost two-thirds of the savings went directly to individuals. This tax cut also helped to build up the economy, to make jobs in industry and to increase the production .of the many things desired to improve the scale of living for the great majority of Americans.

The strong expansion of the economy, coupled with a constant care for efficiency in government operations and an alert guard against waste and duplication, has brought us to a prospective balance between income and expenditure. This is being done while we continue to strengthen our military security.

I expect the budget to be in balance during the fiscal year ending June 30, 1956.

I shall propose a balanced budget for the next fiscal year ending June 30, 1957.

But the balance we are seeking cannot be accomplished without the continuing every-day effort of the Executive and Legislative Branches to keep expenditures under control. It will also be necessary to continue all of the present excise taxes without any reduction and the corporation income taxes at their present rates for another year beyond next April 1st.

It is unquestionably true that our present tax level is very burdensome and, in the interest of long term and continuous economic growth, should be reduced when we prudently can. It is essential, in the sound management of the Government's finances, that we be mindful of our enormous national debt and of the obligation we have toward future Americans to reduce that debt whenever we can appropriately do so. Under conditions of high peacetime prosperity, such as now exist, we can never justify going further into debt to give ourselves a tax cut at the expense of our children. So, in the present state of our financial affairs, I earnestly believe that a tax cut can be deemed justifiable only when it will not unbalance the budget, a budget which makes provision for some reduction, even though modest, in our national debt. In this way we can best maintain fiscal integrity.

A fourth aim of our program is:

TO FOSTER A STRONG ECONOMY

Our competitive enterprise system depends on the energy of free human beings, limited by prudent restraints in law, using free markets to plan, organize and distribute production, and spurred by the prospect of reward for successful effort. This system has developed our resources. It has marvelously expanded our productive capacity. Against the record of all other economic systems devised through the ages, this competitive system has proved the most creative user of human skills in the development of physical resources, and the richest rewarder of human effort.

This is still true in this era when improved living standards and rising national requirements are accompanied by swift advances in technology and rapid obsolescence in machines and methods. Typical of these are the strides made in construction of plants to produce electrical energy from atomic power and of laboratories and installations for the application of this new force in industry, agriculture and the healing arts. These developments make it imperative—to assure effective functioning of our enterprise system—that the Federal Government concern itself with certain broad areas of our economic life. Most important of these is:

Agriculture

Our farm people are not sharing as they should in the general prosperity. They alone of all major groups have seen their incomes decline rather than rise. They are caught between two millstones—rising production costs and declining prices. Such harm to a part of the national economy so vitally important to everyone is of great concern to us all. No other resource is so indispensable as the land that feeds and clothes us. No group is more fundamental to our national life than our farmers.

In successful prosecution of the war, the nation called for the utmost effort of its farmers. Their response was superb, their contribution unsurpassed. Farmers are not now to be blamed for the mountainous, price-depressing surpluses produced in response to wartime policies and laws that were too long continued. War markets are not the markets of peacetime. Failure to recognize that basic fact by a timely adjustment of wartime legislation brought its inevitable result in peacetime— surpluses, lower prices and lower incomes for our farmers.

The dimensions of government responsibility are as broad and complex as the farm problem itself. We are here concerned not only with our essential continuing supplies of food and fiber, but also with a way of life. Both are indispensable to the well-being and strength of the nation. Consideration of these matters must be above and beyond politics. Our national farm policy, so vital to the welfare of farm people and all of us, must not become a field for political warfare. Too much is at stake.

Our farm people expect of us, who have responsibility for their government, understanding of their problems and the will to help solve them. Our objective must be to help bring production into balance with existing and new markets, at prices that yield farmers a return for their work in line with what other Americans get.

To reach this goal, deep-seated problems must be subjected to a stepped-up attack. There is no single easy solution. Rather, there must be a many-sided assault on the stubborn problems of surpluses, prices, costs, and markets; and a steady, persistent, imaginative advance in the relationship between farmers and their government.

In a few days, by special message, I shall lay before the Congress my detailed recommendations for new steps that should be taken promptly to speed the transition in agriculture and thus assist our farmers to achieve their fair share of the national income.

Basic to this program will be a new attack on the surplus problem-for even the best-conceived farm program cannot work under a multi-billion dollar weight of accumulated stocks.

I shall urge authorization of a soil bank program to alleviate the problem of diverted acres and an overexpanded agricultural plant. This will include an acreage reserve to reduce current and accumulated surpluses of crops in most serious difficulty, and a conservation reserve to achieve other needed adjustments in the use of agricultural resources. I shall urge measures to strengthen our surplus disposal activities.

I shall propose measures to strengthen individual commodity programs, to remove controls where possible, to reduce carryovers, and to stop further accumulations of surpluses. I shall ask the Congress to provide substantial new funds for an expanded drive on the research front, to develop new markets, new crops, and new uses. The Rural Development Program to better the lot of low-income farm families deserves full Congressional support. The Great Plains Program must go forward vigorously. Advances on these and other fronts will pull down the pricedepressing surpluses and raise farm income.

In this time of testing in agriculture, we should all together, regardless of party, carry forward resolutely with a sound and forward looking program on which farm people may confidently depend, now and for years to come.

I shall briefly mention four other subjects directly related to the well-being of the economy, preliminary to their fuller discussion in the Economic Report and later communications.

Resources Conservation

I wish to re-emphasize the critical importance of the wise use and conservation of our great natural resources of land, forests, minerals and water and their long-range development consistent with our agricultural policy. Water in particular now plays an increasing role in industrial processes, in the irrigation of land, in electric power, as well as in domestic uses. At the same time, it has the potential of damage and disaster.

A comprehensive legislative program for water conservation will be submitted to the Congress during the Session. The development of our water resources cannot be accomplished overnight. The need is such that we must make faster progress and without delay. Therefore, I strongly recommend that action be taken at this Session on such wholly Federal projects as the Colorado River Storage Project and the Fryingpan-Arkansas Project; on the John Day partnership project, and other projects which provide for cooperative action between the Federal Government and non-Federal interests; and on legislation, which makes provision for Federal participation in small projects under the primary sponsorship of agencies of State and local government.

During the past year the areas of our National Parks have been expanded, and new wildlife refuges have been created. The visits of our people to the Parks have increased much more rapidly than have the facilities to care for them. The Administration will submit recommendations to provide more adequate facilities to keep abreast of the increasing interest of our people in the great outdoors.

Disaster Assistance

A modern community is a complex combination of skills, specialized buildings, machines, communications and homes. Most importantly, it involves human lives. Disaster in many forms—by flood, frost, high winds, for instance—can destroy on a massive scale in a few hours the labor of many years.

Through the past three years the Administration has repeatedly moved into action wherever disaster struck. The extent of State participation in relief activities, however, has been far from uniform and, in many cases, has been either inadequate or nonexistent. Disaster assistance legislation requires overhauling and an experimental program of flood-damage indemnities should be undertaken. The Administration will make detailed recommendations on these subjects.

Area Redevelopment

We must help deal with the pockets of chronic unemployment that here and there mar the nation's general industrial prosperity. Economic changes in recent years have been often so rapid and far-reaching that areas committed to a single local resource or industrial activity have found themselves temporarily deprived of their markets and their livelihood.

Such conditions mean severe hardship for thousands of people as the slow process of adaptation to new circumstances goes on. This process can be speeded up. Last year I authorized a major study of the problem to find additional steps to supplement existing programs for the redevelopment of areas of chronic unemployment. Recommendations will be submitted, designed to supplement, with Federal technical and loan assistance local efforts to get on with this vital job.

Improving such communities must, of course, remain the primary responsibility of the people living there and of their States. But a soundly conceived Federal partnership program can be of real assistance to them in their efforts.

Highway Legislation.

Legislation to provide a modern, interstate highway system is even more urgent this year than last, for 12 months have now passed in which we have fallen further behind in road construction needed for the personal safety, the general prosperity, the national security of the American people. During the year, the number of motor vehicles has increased from 58 to 61 million. During the past year over 38,000 persons lost their lives in highway accidents, while the fearful toll of injuries and property damage has gone on unabated.

In my message of February 22, 1955, I urged that measures be taken to complete the vital 40,000 mile interstate system over a period of 10 years at an estimated Federal cost of approximately 25 billion dollars. No program was adopted.

If we are ever to solve our mounting traffic problem, the whole interstate system must be authorized as one project, to be completed approximately within the specified time. Only in this way can industry efficiently gear itself to the job ahead. Only in this way can the required planning and engineering be accomplished without the confusion and waste unavoidable a piecemeal approach. Furthermore, as I pointed out last year, the pressing nature of this problem must not lead us to solutions outside the bounds of sound fiscal management. As in the case of other pressing problems, there must be an adequate plan of financing. To continue the drastically needed improvement in other national highway systems, I recommend the continuation of the Federal Aid Highway Program.

Aside from agriculture and the four subjects specifically mentioned, an integral part of our efforts to foster a strong and expanding free economy is keeping open the door of opportunity to new and small enterprises, checking monopoly, and preserving a competitive environment. In this past year the steady improvement in the economic health of small business has reinforced the vitality of our competitive economy. We shall continue to help small business concerns to obtain access to adequate financing and to competent counsel on management, production, and marketing problems.

Through measures already taken, opportunities for smallbusiness participation in government procurement programs, including military procurement, are greatly improved. The effectiveness of these measures will become increasingly apparent. We shall continue to make certain that small business has a fair opportunity to compete and has an economic environment in which it may prosper.

In my message last year I referred to the appointment of an advisory committee to appraise and report to me on the deficiencies as well as the effectiveness of existing Federal transportation policies. I have commended the fundamental purposes and objectives of the committee's report. I earnestly recommend that the Congress give prompt attention to the committee's proposals.

Essential to a prosperous economic environment for all business, small and large—for agriculture and industry and commerce-is efficiency in Government. To that end, exhaustive studies of the entire governmental structure were made by the Commission on Intergovernmental Relations and the Commission on the Organization of the Executive Branch of the Government—the reports of these Commissions are now under intensive review and already in the process of implementation in important areas.

One specific and most vital governmental function merits study and action by the Congress. As part of our program of promoting efficiency in Government and getting the fiscal situation in hand, the Post Office Department in the past three years has been overhauled. Nearly one thousand new post offices have been provided. Financial practices have been modernized, and transportation and operating methods are being constantly improved. A new wage and incentive plan for the half million postal employees has been established. Never before has the postal system handled so much mail so quickly and so economically.

The Post Office Department faces two serious problems. First, much of its physical plant—post offices and other buildings-is obsolete and inadequate. Many new buildings and the modernization of present ones are essential if we are to have improved mail service. The second problem is the Department's fiscal plight. It now faces an annual deficit of one-half billion dollars.

Recommendations on postal facilities and on additional postal revenues will be submitted to the Congress.

A final consideration in our program planning is:

THE RESPONSE TO HUMAN CONCERNS

A fundamental belief shines forth in this Republic. We believe in the worth and dignity of the individual. We know that if we are to govern ourselves wisely—in the tradition of America—we must have the opportunity to develop our individual capacities to the utmost.

To fulfill the individual's aspirations in the American way of life, good education is fundamental. Good education is the outgrowth of good homes, good communities, good churches, and good schools. Today our schools face pressing problems—problems which will not yield to swift and easy solutions, or to any single action. They will yield only to a continuing, active, formed effort by the people toward achieving better schools.

This kind of effort has been spurred by the thousands of conferences held in recent months by half a million citizens and educators in all parts of the country, culminating in the White House Conference on Education. In that Conference, some two thousand delegates, broadly representative of the nation, studied together the problems of the nation's schools.

They concluded that the people of the United States must make a greater effort through their local, State, and Federal Governments to improve the education of our youth. This expression from the people must now be translated into action at all levels of government.

So far as the Federal share of responsibility is concerned, I urge that the Congress move promptly to enact an effective program of Federal assistance to help erase the existing deficit of school classrooms. Such a program, which should be limited to a five-year period, must operate to increase rather than decrease local and State support of schools and to give the greatest help to the States and localities with the least financial resources. Federal aid should in no way jeopardize the freedom of local school systems. There will be presented to the Congress a recommended program of Federal assistance for school construction.

Such a program should be accompanied by action to increase services to the nation's schools by the Office of Education and by legislation to provide continuation of payments to school districts where Federal activities have impaired the ability of those districts to provide adequate schools.

Under the 1954 Amendments to the old-age and survivors' insurance program, protection was extended to some 10 million additional workers and benefits were increased. The system now helps protect 9 out of 10 American workers and their families against loss of income in old age or on the death of the breadwinner. The system is sound. It must be kept so. In developing improvements in the system, we must give the most careful consideration to population and social trends, and to fiscal requirements. With these considerations in mind, the Administration will present its recommendations for further expansion of coverage and other steps which can be taken wisely at this time.

Other needs in the area of social welfare include increased child welfare services, extension of the program of aid to dependent children, intensified attack on juvenile delinquency, and special attention to the problems of mentally retarded children. The training of more skilled workers for these fields and the quest for new knowledge through research in social welfare are essential. Similarly the problems of our aged people need our attention.

The nation has made dramatic progress in conquering disease—progress of profound human significance which can be greatly accelerated by an intensified effort in medical research. A well-supported, well-balanced program of research, including basic research, can open new frontiers of knowledge, prevent and relieve suffering, and prolong life. Accordingly I shall recommend a substantial increase in Federal funds for the support of such a program. As an integral part of this effort, I shall recommend a new plan to aid construction of non-Federal medical research and teaching facilities and to help provide more adequate support for the training of medical research manpower.

Finally, we must aid in cushioning the heavy and rising costs of illness and hospitalization to individuals and families. Provision should be made, by Federal reinsurance or otherwise, to foster extension of voluntary health insurance coverage to many more persons, especially older persons and those in rural areas. Plans should be evolved to improve protection against the costs of prolonged or severe illness. These measures will help reduce the dollar barrier between many Americans and the benefits of modern medical care.

The Administration health program will be submitted to the Congress in detail.

The response of government to human concerns embraces, of course, other measures of broad public interest, and of special interest to our working men and women. The need still exists for improvement of the Labor Management Relations Act. The recommendations I submitted to the Congress last year take into account not only the interests of labor and management but also the public welfare. The needed amendments should be enacted without further delay.

We must also carry forward the job of improving the wagehour law. Last year I requested the Congress to broaden the coverage of the minimum wage. I repeat that recommendation, and I pledge the full resources of the Executive Branch to assist the Congress in finding ways to attain this goal. Moreover, as requested last year, legislation should be passed to clarify and strengthen the eight-hour laws for the benefit of workers who are subject to Federal wage standards on Federal and Federally assisted construction and other public works.

The Administration will shortly propose legislation to assure adequate disclosure of the financial affairs of each employee pension and welfare plan and to afford substantial protection to their beneficiaries in accordance with the objectives outlined in my message of January 11, 1954. Occupational safety still demands attention, as I pointed out last year, and legislation to improve the Longshoremen's and Harbor Workers' Compensation Act is still needed. The improvement of the District of Columbia Unemployment Insurance Law and legislation to provide employees in the District with non-occupational disability insurance are no less necessary now than 12 months ago. Legislation to apply the principle of equal pay for equal work without discrimination because of sex is a matter of simple justice. I earnestly urge the Congress to move swiftly to implement these needed labor measures.

In the field of human needs, we must carry forward the housing program, which is contributing so greatly to the well-being of our people and the prosperity of our economy. Home ownership is now advanced to the point where almost three of every five families in our cities, towns, and suburbs own the houses they live in.

For the housing program, most of the legislative authority already exists. However, a firm program of public housing is essential until the private building industry has found ways to provide more adequate housing for low-income families. The Administration will propose authority to contract for 35 thousand additional public housing units in each of the next 2 fiscal years for communities which will participate in an integrated attack on slums and blight.

To meet the needs of the growing number of older people, several amendments to the National Housing Act will be proposed to assist the private homebuilding industry as well as charitable and non-profit organizations.

With so large a number of the American people desiring to modernize and improve existing dwellings, I recommend that the Title 1 program for permanent improvements in the home be liberalized.

I recommend increases in the general FHA mortgage insurance authority; the extension of the FHA military housing program; an increase in the authorization for Urban Planning grants; in the special assistance authority of the Federal National Mortgage Association; and continued support of the college housing program in a way that will not discourage private capital from helping to meet the needs of our colleges.

The legislation I have recommended for workers in private industry should be accompanied by a parallel effort for the welfare of Government employees. We have accomplished much in this field, including a contributory life insurance program; equitable pay increases and a fringe benefits program, covering many needed personnel policy changes, from improved premium pay to a meaningful incentive award program.

Additional personnel management legislation is needed in this Session. As I stated last year, an executive pay increase is essential to efficient governmental management. Such an increase, together with needed adjustments in the pay for the top career positions, is also necessary to the equitable completion of the Federal pay program initiated last year. Other legislation will be proposed, including legislation for prepaid group health insurance for employees and their dependents and to effect major improvements in the Civil Service retirement system.

All of us share a continuing concern for those who have served this nation in the Armed Forces. The Commission on Veterans Pensions is at this time conducting a study of the entire field of veterans' benefits and will soon submit proposed improvements.

We are proud of the progress our people have made in the field of civil rights. In Executive Branch operations through-out the nation, elimination of discrimination and segregation is all but completed. Progress is also being made among contractors engaged in furnishing Government services and requirements. Every citizen now has the opportunity to fit himself for and to hold a position of responsibility in the service of his country. In the District of Columbia, through the voluntary cooperation of the people, discrimination and segregation are disappearing from hotels, theaters, restaurants and other facilities.

It is disturbing that in some localities allegations persist that Negro citizens are being deprived of their right to vote and are likewise being subjected to unwarranted economic pressures. I recommend that the substance of these charges be thoroughly examined by a Bipartisan Commission created by the Congress. It is hoped that such a commission will be established promptly so that it may arrive at findings which can receive early consideration.

The stature of our leadership in the free world has increased through the past three years because we have made more progress than ever before in a similar period to assure our citizens equality in justice, in opportunity and in civil rights. We must expand this effort on every front. We must strive to have every person judged and measured by what he is, rather than by his color, race or religion. There will soon be recommended to the Congress a program further to advance the efforts of the Government, within the area of Federal responsibility, to accomplish these objectives.

One particular challenge confronts us. In the Hawaiian Islands, East meets West. To the Islands, Asia and Europe and the Western Hemisphere, all the continents, have contributed their peoples and their cultures to display a unique example of a community that is a successful laboratory in human brotherhood.

Statehood, supported by the repeatedly expressed desire of the Islands' people and by our traditions, would be a shining example of the American way to the entire earth. Consequently, I urgently request this Congress to grant statehood for Hawaii. Also, in harmony with the provisions I last year communicated to the Senate and House Committees on Interior and Insular Affairs, I trust that progress toward statehood for Alaska can be made in this Session.

Progress is constant toward full integration of our Indian citizens into normal community life. During the past two years the Administration has provided school facilities for thousands of Indian children previously denied this opportunity. We must continue to meet the needs of increased numbers of Indian children. Provision should also be made for the education of adult Indians whose schooling in earlier years was neglected.

In keeping with our responsibility of world leadership and in our own self interest, I again point out to the Congress the urgent need for revision of the immigration and nationality laws. Our nation has always welcomed immigrants to our shores. The wisdom of such a policy is clearly shown by the fact that America has been built by immigrants and the descendants of immigrants. That policy must be continued realistically with present day conditions in mind.

I recommend that the number of persons admitted to this country annually be based not on the 1920 census but on the latest, the 1950 census. Provision should be made to allow for greater flexibility in the use of quotas so if one country does not use its share, the vacancies may be made available for the use of qualified individuals from other countries.

The law should be amended to permit the Secretary of State and the Attorney General to waive the requirements of fingerprinting on a reciprocal basis for persons coming to this country for temporary visits. This and other changes in the law are long overdue and should be taken care of promptly. Detailed recommendations for revision of the immigration laws will be submitted to the Congress.

I am happy to report substantial progress in the flow of immigrants under the Refugee Relief Act of 1953; however, I again request this Congress to approve without further delay the urgently needed amendments to that act which I submitted in the last Session. Because of the high prosperity in Germany and Austria, the number of immigrants from those countries will be reduced. This will make available thousands of unfilled openings which I recommend be distributed to Greece and Italy and to escapees from behind the Iron Curtain.

Once again I ask the Congress to join with me in demonstrating our belief in the right of suffrage. I renew my request that the principle of self-government be extended and the right of suffrage granted to the citizens of the District of Columbia.

To conclude: the vista before us is bright. The march of science, the expanding economy, the advance in collective security toward a just peace—in this threefold movement our people are creating new standards by which the future of the Republic may be judged.

Progress, however, will be realized only as it is more than matched by a continuing growth in the spiritual strength of the nation. Our dedication to moral values must be complete in our dealings abroad and in our relationships among ourselves. We have single-minded devotion to the common good of America. Never must we forget that this means the well-being, the prosperity, the security of all Americans in every walk of life.

To the attainment of these objectives, I pledge full energies of the Administration, as in the Session ahead, it works on a program for submission to you, the Congress of the United States.

2.5   Dwight D. Eisenhower's Fifth State of the Union Address

To the Congress of the United States:

I appear before the Congress today to report on the State of the Union and the relationships of the Union to the other nations of the world. I come here, firmly convinced that at no time in the history of the Republic have circumstances more emphatically underscored the need, in all echelons of government, for vision and wisdom and resolution.

You meet in a season of stress that is testing the fitness of political systems and the validity of political philosophies. Each stress stems in part from causes peculiar to itself. But every stress is a reflection of a universal phenomenon.

In the world today, the surging and understandable tide of nationalism is marked by widespread revulsion and revolt against tyranny, injustice, inequality and poverty. As individuals, joined in a common hunger for freedom, men and women and even children pit their spirit against guns and tanks. On a larger scale, in an ever more persistent search for the self-respect of authentic sovereignty and the economic base on which national independence must rest, peoples sever old ties; seek new alliances; experiment—sometimes dangerously—in their struggle to satisfy these human aspirations.

Particularly, in the past year, this tide has changed the pattern of attitudes and thinking among millions. The changes already accomplished foreshadow a world transformed by the spirit of freedom. This is no faint and pious hope. The forces now at work in the minds and hearts of men will not be spent through. many years. In the main, today's expressions of nationalism are, in spirit, echoes of our forefathers' struggle for independence.

This Republic cannot be aloof to these events heralding a new epoch in the affairs of mankind.

Our pledged word, our enlightened self-interest, our character as a Nation commit us to a high role in world affairs: a role of vigorous leadership, ready strength, sympathetic understanding.

The State of the Union, at the opening of the 85th Congress continues to vindicate the wisdom of the principles on which this Republic is rounded. Proclaimed in the Constitution of the Nation and in many of our historic documents, and rounded in devout religious convictions, these principles enunciate:

A vigilant regard for human liberty.

A wise concern for human welfare.

A ceaseless effort for human progress.

Fidelity to these principles, in our relations with other peoples, has won us new friendships and has increased our opportunity for service within the family of nations. The appeal of these principles is universal, lighting fires in the souls of men everywhere. We shall continue to uphold them, against those who deny them and in counselling with our friends.

At home, the application of these principles to the complex problems of our national life has brought us to an unprecedented peak in our economic prosperity and has exemplified in our way of life the enduring human values of mind and spirit.

Through the past four years these principles have guided the legislative programs submitted by the Administration to the Congress. As we attempt to apply them to current events, domestic and foreign, we must take into account the complex entity that is the United States of America; what endangers it; what can improve it.

The visible structure is our American economy itself. After more than a century and a half of constant expansion, it is still rich in a wide variety of natural resources. It is first among nations in its people'.s mastery of industrial skills. It is productive beyond our own needs of many foodstuffs and industrial products. It is rewarding to all our citizens in opportunity to earn and to advance in self-realization and in self-expression. It is fortunate in its wealth of educational and cultural and religious centers. It is vigorously dynamic in the limitless initiative and willingness to venture that characterize free enterprise. It is productive of a widely shared prosperity.

Our economy is strong, expanding, and fundamentally sound. But in any realistic appraisal, even the optimistic analyst will realize that in a prosperous period the principal threat to efficient functioning of a free enterprise system is inflation. We look back on four years of prosperous activities during which prices, the cost of living, have been relatively stable—that is, inflation has been held in check. But it is clear that the danger is always present, particularly if the government might become profligate in its expenditures or private groups might ignore all the possible results on our economy of unwise struggles for immediate gain.

This danger requires a firm resolution that the Federal Government shall utilize only a prudent share of the Nation's resources, that it shall live within its means, carefully measuring against need alternative proposals for expenditures.

Through the next four years, I shall continue to insist that the executive departments and agencies of Government search out additional ways to save money and manpower. I urge that the Congress be equally watchful in this matter.

We pledge the Government's share in guarding the integrity of the dollar. But the Government's efforts cannot be the entire campaign against inflation, the thief that can rob the individual of the value of the pension and social security he has earned during his productive life. For success, Government's efforts must be paralleled by the attitudes and actions of individual citizens.

I have often spoken of the purpose of this Administration to serve the national interest of 170 million people. The national interest must take precedence over temporary advantages which may be secured by particular groups at the expense of all the people.

In this regard I call on leaders in business and in labor to think well on their responsibility to the American people. With all elements of our society, they owe the Nation a vigilant guard against the inflationary tendencies that are always at work in a dynamic economy operating at today's high levels. They can powerfully help counteract or accentuate such tendencies by their wage and price policies.

Business in its pricing policies should avoid unnecessary price increases especially at a time like the present when demand in so many areas presses hard on short supplies. A reasonable profit is essential to the new investments that provide more jobs in an expanding economy. But business leaders must, in the national interest, studiously avoid those price rises that are possible only because of vital or unusual needs of the whole nation.

If our economy is to remain healthy, increases in wages and other labor benefits, negotiated by labor and management, must be reasonably related to improvements in productivity. Such increases are beneficial, for they provide wage earners with greater purchasing power. Except where necessary to correct obvious injustices, wage increases that outrun productivity, however, are an inflationary factor. They make for higher prices for the public generally and impose a particular hardship on those whose welfare depends on the purchasing power of retirement income and savings. Wage negotiations should also take cognizance of the right of the public generally to share in the benefits of improvements in technology.

Freedom has been defined as the opportunity for self-discipline. This definition has a special application to the areas of wage and price policy in a free economy. Should we persistently fail to discipline ourselves, eventually there will be increasing pressure on government to redress the failure. By that process freedom will step by step disappear. No subject on the domestic scene should more attract the concern of the friends of American working men and women and of free business enterprise than the forces that threaten a steady depreciation of the value of our money.

Concerning developments in another vital sector of our economy—agriculture—I am gratified that the long slide in farm income has been halted and that further improvement is in prospect. This is heartening progress. Three tools that we have developed—improved surplus disposal, improved price support laws, and the soil bank—are working to reduce price-depressing government stocks of farm products. Our concern for the well-being of farm families demands that we constantly search for new ways by which they can share more fully in our unprecedented prosperity. Legislative recommendations in the field of agriculture are contained in the Budget Message.

Our soil, water, mineral, forest, fish, and wildlife resources are being conserved and improved more effectively. Their conservation and development are vital to the present and future strength of the Nation. But they must not be the concern of the Federal Government alone. State and local entities, and private enterprise should be encouraged to participate in such projects.

I would like to make special mention of programs for making the best uses of water, rapidly becoming our most precious natural resource, just as it can be, when neglected, a destroyer of both life and wealth. There has been prepared and published a comprehensive water report developed by a Cabinet Committee and relating to all phases of this particular problem.

In the light of this report, there are two things I believe we should keep constantly in mind. The first is that each of our great river valleys should be considered as a whole. Piecemeal operations within each lesser drainage area can be self-defeating or, at the very least, needlessly expensive. The second is that the domestic and industrial demands for water grow far more rapidly than does our population.

The whole matter of making the best use of each drop of water from the moment it touches our soil until it reaches the oceans, for such purposes as irrigation, flood control, power production, and domestic and industrial uses clearly demands the closest kind of cooperation and partnership between municipalities, States and the Federal Government. Through partnership of Federal, state and local authorities in these vast projects we can obtain the economy and efficiency of development and operation that springs from a lively sense of local responsibility.

Until such partnership is established on a proper and logical basis of sharing authority, responsibility and costs, our country will never have both the fully productive use of water that it so obviously needs and protection against disastrous flood.

If we fail in this, all the many tasks that need to be done in America could be accomplished only at an excessive cost, by the growth of a stifling bureaucracy, and eventually with a dangerous degree of centralized control over our national life.

In all domestic matters, I believe that the people of the United States will expect of us effective action to remedy past failure in meeting critical needs.

High priority should be given the school construction bill. This will benefit children of all races throughout the country-and children of all races need schools now. A program designed to meet emergency needs for more classrooms should be enacted without delay. I am hopeful that this program can be enacted on its own merits, uncomplicated by provisions dealing with the complex problems of integration. I urge the people in all sections of the country to approach these problems with calm and reason, with mutual understanding and good will, and in the American tradition of deep respect for the orderly processes of law and justice.

I should say here that we have much reason to be proud of the progress our people are making in mutual understanding— the chief buttress of human and civil rights. Steadily we are moving closer to the goal of fair and equal treatment of citizens without regard to race or color. But unhappily much remains to be done.

Last year the Administration recommended to the Congress a four-point program to reinforce civil rights. That program included:

(1) creation of a bipartisan commission to investigate asserted violations of civil rights and to make recommendations;

(2) creation of a civil rights division in the Department of Justice in charge of an Assistant Attorney General;

(3) enactment by the Congress of new laws to aid in the enforcement of voting rights; and

(4) amendment of the laws so as to permit the Federal Government to seek from the civil courts preventive relief in civil rights cases.

I urge that the Congress enact this legislation.

Essential to the stable economic growth we seek is a system of well-adapted and efficient financial institutions. I believe the time has come to conduct a broad national inquiry into the nature, performance and adequacy of our financial system, both in terms of its direct service to the whole economy and in terms of its function as the mechanism through which monetary and credit policy takes effect. I believe the Congress should authorize the creation of a commission of able and qualified citizens to undertake this vital inquiry. Out of their findings and recommendations the Administration would develop and present to the Congress any legislative proposals that might be indicated for the purpose of improving our financial machinery.

In this message it seems unnecessary that I should repeat recommendations involving our domestic affairs that have been urged upon the Congress during the past four years, but which, in some instances, did not reach the stage of completely satisfactory legislation.

The Administration will, through future messages either directly from me or from heads of the departments and agencies, transmit to the Congress specific recommendations. These will involve our financial and fiscal affairs, our military and civil defenses; the administration of justice; our agricultural economy; our domestic and foreign commerce; the urgently needed increase in our postal rates; the development of our natural resources; our labor laws, including our labor-management relations legislation, and vital aspects of the health, education and welfare of our people. There will be special recommendations dealing with such subjects as atomic energy, the furthering of public works, the continued efforts to eliminate government competition with the businesses of tax-paying citizens.

A number of legislative recommendations will be mentioned specifically in my forthcoming Budget Message, which will reach you within the week. That message will also recommend such sums as are needed to implement the proposed action.

Turning to the international scene:

The existence of a strongly armed imperialistic dictatorship poses a continuing threat to the free world's and thus to our own Nation's security and peace. There are certain truths to be remembered here.

First, America alone and isolated cannot assure even its own security. We must be joined by the capability and resolution of nations that have proved themselves dependable defenders of freedom. Isolation from them invites war. Our security is also enhanced by the immeasurable interest that joins us with all peoples who believe that peace with justice must be preserved, that wars of aggression are crimes against humanity.

Another truth is that our survival in today's world requires modern, adequate, dependable military strength. Our Nation has made great strides in assuring a modern defense, so armed in new weapons, so deployed, so equipped, that today our security force is the most powerful in our peacetime history. It can punish heavily any enemy who undertakes to attack us. It is a major deterrent to war.

By our research and development more efficient weapons-some of amazing capabilities—are being constantly created. These vital efforts we shall continue. Yet we must not delude ourselves that safety necessarily increases as expenditures for military research or forces in being go up. Indeed, beyond a wise and reasonable level, which is always changing and is under constant study, money spent on arms may be money wasted on sterile metal or inflated costs, thereby weakening the very security and strength we seek.

National security requires far more than military power. Economic and moral factors play indispensable roles. Any program that endangers our economy could defeat us. Any weakening of our national will and resolution, any diminution of the vigor and initiative of our individual citizens, would strike a blow at the heart of our defenses.

The finest military establishment we can produce must work closely in cooperation with the forces of our friends. Our system of regional pacts, developed within the Charter of the United Nations, serves to increase both our own security and the security of other nations.

This system is still a recent introduction on the world scene. Its problems are many and difficult, because it insists on equality among its members and brings into association some nations traditionally divided. Repeatedly in recent months, the collapse of these regional alliances has been predicted. The strains upon them have been at times indeed severe. Despite these strains our regional alliances have proved durable and strong, and dire predictions of their disintegration have proved completely false.

With other free nations, we should vigorously prosecute measures that will promote mutual strength, prosperity and welfare within the free world. Strength is essentially a product of economic health and social well-being. Consequently, even as we continue our programs of military assistance, we must emphasize aid to our friends in building more productive economies and in better satisfying the natural demands of their people for progress. Thereby we shall move a long way toward a peaceful world.

A sound and safeguarded agreement for open skies, unarmed aerial sentinels, and reduced armament would provide a valuable contribution toward a durable peace in the years ahead. And we have been persistent in our effort to reach such an agreement. We are willing to enter any reliable agreement which would reverse the trend toward ever more devastating nuclear weapons; reciprocally provide against the possibility of surprise attack; mutually control the outer space missile and satellite development; and make feasible a lower level of armaments and armed forces and an easier burden of military expenditures. Our continuing negotiations in this field are a major part of our quest for a confident peace in this atomic age.

This quest requires as well a constructive attitude among all the nations of the free world toward expansion of trade and investment, that can give all of us opportunity to work out economic betterment.

An essential step in this field is the provision of an administrative agency to insure the orderly and proper operation of existing arrangements trader which multilateral trade is now carried on. To that end I urge Congressional authorization for United States membership in the proposed Organization for Trade Cooperation, an action which will speed removal of discrimination against our export trade.

We welcome the efforts of a number of our European friends to achieve an integrated community to develop a common market. We likewise welcome their cooperative effort in the field of atomic energy.

To demonstrate once again our unalterable purpose to make of the atom a peaceful servant of humanity, I shortly shall ask the Congress to authorize full United States participation in the International Atomic Energy Agency.

World events have magnified both the responsibilities and the opportunities of the United States Information Agency. Just as, in recent months, the voice of communism has become more shaken and confused, the voice of truth must be more clearly heard. To enable our Information Agency to cope with these new responsibilities and opportunities, I am asking the Congress to increase appreciably the appropriations for this program and for legislation establishing a career service for the Agency's overseas foreign service officers.

The recent historic events in Hungary demand that all free nations share to the extent of their capabilities in the responsibility of granting asylum to victims of Communist persecution. I request the Congress promptly to enact legislation to regularize the status in the United States of Hungarian refugees brought here as parolees. I shall shortly recommend to the Congress by special message the changes in our immigration laws that I deem necessary in the light of our world responsibilities.

The cost of peace is something we must face boldly, fearlessly. Beyond money, it involves changes in attitudes, the renunciation of old prejudices, even the sacrifice of some seeming self-interest.

Only five days ago I expressed to you the grave concern of your Government over the threat of Soviet aggression in the Middle East. I asked for Congressional authorization to help counter this threat. I say again that this matter is of vital and immediate importance to the Nation's and the free world's security and peace. By our proposed programs in the Middle East, we hope to assist in establishing a climate in which constructive and long-term solutions to basic problems of the area may be sought.

From time to time, there will be presented to the Congress requests for other legislation in the broad field of international affairs. All requests will reflect the steadfast purpose of this Administration to pursue peace, based on justice. Although in some cases details will be new, the underlying purpose and objectives will remain the same.

All proposals made by the Administration in this field are based on the free world's unity. This unity may not be immediately obvious unless we examine link by link the chain of relationships that binds us to every area and to every nation. In spirit the free world is one because its people uphold the right of independent existence for all nations. I have already alluded to their economic interdependence. But their interdependence extends also into the field of security.

First of all, no reasonable man will question the absolute need for our American neighbors to be prosperous and secure. Their security and prosperity are inextricably bound to our own. And we are, of course, already joined with these neighbors by historic pledges.

Again, no reasonable man will deny that the freedom and prosperity and security of Western Europe are vital to our own prosperity and security. If the institutions, the skills, the manpower of its peoples were to fall under the domination of an aggressive imperialism, the violent change in the balance of world power and in the pattern of world commerce could not be fully compensated for by any American measures, military or economic.

But these people, whose economic strength is largely dependent on free and uninterrupted movement of oil from the Middle East, cannot prosper—indeed, their economies would be severely impaired—should that area be controlled by an enemy and the movement of oil be subject to its decisions.

Next, to the Eastward, are Asiatic and Far Eastern peoples, recently returned to independent control of their own affairs or now emerging into sovereign statehood. Their potential strength constitutes new assurance for stability and peace in the world—if they can retain their independence. Should they lose freedom and be dominated by an aggressor, the world-wide effects would imperil the security of the free world.

In short, the world has so shrunk that all free nations are our neighbors. Without cooperative neighbors, the United States cannot maintain its own security and welfare, because:

First, America's vital interests are world-wide, embracing both hemispheres and every continent.

Second, we have community of interest with every nation in the free world.

Third, interdependence of interests requires a decent respect for the rights and the peace of all peoples.

These principles motivate our actions within the United Nations. There, before all the world, by our loyalty to them, by our practice of them, let us strive to set a standard to which all who seek justice and who hunger for peace can rally.

May we at home, here at the Seat of Government, in all the cities and towns and farmlands of America, support these principles in a personal effort of dedication. Thereby each of us can help establish a secure world order in which opportunity for freedom and justice will be more widespread, and in which the resources now dissipated on the armaments of war can be released for the life and growth of all humanity.

When our forefathers prepared the immortal document that proclaimed our independence, they asserted that every individual is endowed by his Creator with certain inalienable rights. As we gaze back through history to that date, it is clear that our nation has striven to live up to this declaration, applying it to nations as well as to individuals.

Today we proudly assert that the government of the United States is still committed to this concept, both in its activities at home and abroad.

The purpose is Divine; the implementation is human.

Our country and its government have made mistakes—human mistakes. They have been of the head—not of the heart. And it is still true that the great concept of the dignity of all men, alike created in the image of the Almighty, has been the compass by which we have tried and are trying to steer our course.

So long as we continue by its guidance, there will be true progress in human affairs, both among ourselves and among those with whom we deal.

To achieve a more perfect fidelity to it, I submit, is a worthy ambition as we meet together in these first days of this, the first session of the 85th Congress.

2.6 Dwight D. Eisenhower's Sixth State of the Union Address

Mr. President, Mr. Speaker, Members of the 85th Congress:

It is again my high privilege to extend personal greetings to the members of the 85th Congress.

All of us realize that, as this new session begins, many Americans are troubled about recent world developments which they believe may threaten our nation's safety. Honest men differ in their appraisal of America's material and intellectual strength, and the dangers that confront us. But all know these dangers are real.

The purpose of this message is to outline the measures that can give the American people a confidence—just as real—in their own security.

I am not here to justify the past, gloss over the problems of the present, or propose easy solutions for the future.

I am here to state what I believe to be right and what I believe to be wrong; and to propose action for correcting what I think wrong!

I.

There are two tasks confronting us that so far outweigh all other that I shall devote this year's message entirely to them. The first is to ensure our safety through strength.

As to our strength, I have repeatedly voiced this conviction: We now have a broadly based and efficient defensive strength, including a great deterrent power, which is, for the present, our main guarantee against war; but, unless we act wisely and promptly, we could lose that capacity to deter attack or defend ourselves.

My profoundest conviction is that the American people will say, as one man: No matter what the exertions or sacrifices, we shall maintain that necessary strength !

But we could make no more tragic mistake than merely to concentrate on military strength. For if we did only this, the future would hold nothing for the world but an Age of Terror.

And so our second task is to do the constructive work of building a genuine peace. We must never become so preoccupied with our desire for military strength that we neglect those areas of economic development, trade, diplomacy, education, ideas and principles where the foundations of real peace must be laid.

II.

The threat to our safety, and to the hope of a peaceful world, can be simply stated. It is communist imperialism.

This threat is not something imagined by critics of the Soviets. Soviet spokesmen, from the beginning, have publicly and frequently declared their aim to expand their power, one way or another, throughout the world.

The threat has become increasingly serious as this expansionist aim has been reinforced by an advancing industrial, military and scientific establishment.

But what makes the Soviet threat unique in history is its all—inclusiveness. Every human activity is pressed into service as a weapon of expansion. Trade, economic development, military power, arts, science, education, the whole world of ideas—all are harnessed to this same chariot of expansion. The Soviets are, in short, waging total cold war.

The only answer to a regime that wages total cold war is to wage total peace. This means bringing to bear every asset of our personal and national lives upon the task of building the conditions in which security and peace can grow.

III.

Among our assets, let us first briefly glance at our military power. Military power serves the cause of security by making prohibitive the cost of any aggressive attack.

It serves the cause of peace by holding up a shield behind which the patient constructive work of peace can go on.

But it can serve neither cause if we make either of two mistakes. The one would be to overestimate our strength, and thus neglect crucially important actions in the period just ahead. The other would be to underestimate our strength. Thereby we might be tempted to become irresolute in our foreign relations, to dishearten our friends, and to lose our national poise and perspective in approaching the complex problems ahead.

Any orderly balance-sheet of military strength must be in two parts. The first is the position as of today. The second is the position in the period ahead.

As of today: our defensive shield comprehends a vast complex of ground, sea, and air units, superbly equipped and strategically deployed around the world. The most powerful deterrent to war in the world today lies in the retaliatory power of our Strategic Air Command and the aircraft of our Navy. They present to any potential attacker who would unleash war upon the world the prospect of virtual annihilation of his own country.

Even if we assume a surprise attack on our bases, with a marked reduction in our striking power, our bombers would immediately be on their way in sufficient strength to accomplish this mission of retaliation. Every informed government knows this. It is no secret.

Since the Korean Armistice, the American people have spent $225 billion in maintaining and strengthening this overall defensive shield. This is the position as of today.

Now as to the period ahead: Every part of our military establishment must and will be equipped to do its defensive job with the most modern weapons and methods. But it is particularly important to our planning that we make a candid estimate of the effect of long-range ballistic missiles on the present deterrent power I have described.

At this moment, the consensus of opinion is that we are probably somewhat behind the Soviets in some areas of long-range ballistic missile development. But it is my conviction, based on close study of all relevant intelligence, that if we make the necessary effort, we will have the missiles, in the needed quantity and in time, to sustain and strengthen the deterrent power of our increasingly efficient bombers. One encouraging fact evidencing this ability is the rate of progress we have achieved since we began to concentrate on these missiles.

The intermediate ballistic missiles, Thor and Jupiter, have already been ordered into production. The parallel progress in the intercontinental ballistic missile effort will be advanced by our plans for acceleration. The development of the submarine-based Polaris missile system has progressed so well that its future procurement schedules are being moved forward markedly.

When it is remembered that our country has concentrated on the development of ballistic missiles for only about a third as long as the Soviets, these achievements show a rate of progress that speaks for itself. Only a brief time back, we were spending at the rate of only about one million dollars a year on long range ballistic missiles. In 1957 we spent more than one billion dollars on the Arias, Titan, Thor, Jupiter, and Polaris programs alone.

But I repeat, gratifying though this rate of progress is, we must still do more!

Our real problem, then, is not our strength today; it is rather the vital necessity of action today to ensure our strength tomorrow.

What I have just said applies to our strength as a single country. But we are not alone. I have returned from the recent NATO meeting with renewed conviction that, because we are a part of a world-wide community of free and peaceful nations, our own security is immeasurably increased.

By contrast, the Soviet Union has surrounded itself with captive and sullen nations. Like a crack in the crust of an uneasily sleeping volcano, the Hungarian uprising revealed the depth and intensity of the patriotic longing for liberty that still burns within these countries.

The world thinks of us as a country which is strong, but which will never start a war. The world also thinks of us as a land which has never enslaved anyone and which is animated by humane ideals. This friendship, based on common ideals, is one of our greatest sources of strength.

It cements into a cohesive security arrangement the aggregate of the spiritual, military and economic strength of all those nations which, with us, are allied by treaties and agreements.

Up to this point, I have talked solely about our military strength to deter a possible future war. I now want to talk about the strength we need to win a different kind of war—one that has already been launched against us.

It is the massive economic offensive that has been mounted by the communist imperialists against free nations.

The communist imperialist regimes have for some time been largely frustrated in their attempts at expansion based directly on force. As a result, they have begun to concentrate heavily on economic penetration, particularly of newly-developing countries, as a preliminary to political domination.

This non-military drive, if underestimated, could defeat the free world regardless of our military strength. This danger is all the greater precisely because many of us fail or refuse to recognize it. Thus, some people may be tempted to finance our extra military effort by cutting economic assistance. But at the very time when the economic threat is assuming menacing proportions, to fail to strengthen our own effort would be nothing less than reckless folly !

Admittedly, most of us did not anticipate the psychological impact upon the world of the launching of the first earth satellite. Let us not make the same kind of mistake in another field, by failing to anticipate the much more serious impact of the Soviet economic offensive.

As with our military potential, our economic assets are more than equal to the task. Our independent farmers produce an abundance of food and fibre. Our free workers are versatile, intelligent, and hardworking. Our businessmen are imaginative and resourceful. The productivity, the adaptability of the American economy is the solid foundation-stone of our security structure.

We have just concluded another prosperous year. Our output was once more the greatest in the nation's history. In the latter part of the year, some decline in employment and output occurred, following the exceptionally rapid expansion of recent years. In a free economy, reflecting as it does the independent judgments of millions of people, growth typically moves forward unevenly. But the basic forces of growth remain unimpaired. There are solid grounds for confidence that economic growth will be resumed without an extended interruption. Moreover, the Federal government, constantly alert to signs of weakening in any part of our economy, always stands ready, with its full power, to take any appropriate further action to promote renewed business expansion.

If our history teaches us anything, it is this lesson: so far as the economic potential of our nation is concerned, the believers in the future of America have always been the realists. I count myself as one of this company.

Our long-range problem, then, is not the stamina of our enormous engine of production. Our problem is to make sure that we use these vast economic forces confidently and creatively, not only in direct military defense efforts, but likewise in our foreign policy, through such activities as mutual economic aid and foreign trade.

In much the same way, we have tremendous potential resources on other non-military fronts to help in countering the Soviet threat: education, science, research, and, not least, the ideas and principles by which we live. And in all these cases the task ahead is to bring these resources more sharply to bear upon the new tasks of security and peace in a swiftly-changing world.

IV.

There are many items in the Administration's program, of a kind frequently included in a State of the Union Message, with which I am not dealing today. They are important to us and to our prosperity. But I am reserving them for treatment in separate communications because of my purpose today of speaking only about matters bearing directly upon our security and peace.

I now place before you an outline of action designed to focus our resources upon the two tasks of security and peace.

In this special category I list eight items requiring action. They are not merely desirable. They are imperative.

1. DEFENSE REORGANIZATION

The first need is to assure ourselves that military organization facilitates rather than hinders the functioning of the military establishment in maintaining the security of the nation.

Since World War II, the purpose of achieving maximum organizational efficiency in a modern defense establishment has several times occasioned action by the Congress and by the Executive.

The advent of revolutionary new devices, bringing with them the problem of overall continental defense, creates new difficulties, reminiscent of those attending the advent of the airplane half a century ago.

Some of the important new weapons which technology has produced do not fit into any existing service pattern. They cut across all services, involve all services, and transcend all services, at every stage from development to operation. In some instances they defy classification according to branch of service.

Unfortunately, the uncertainties resulting from such a situation, and the jurisdictional disputes attending upon it, tend to bewilder and confuse the public and create the impression that service differences are damaging the national interest.

Let us proudly remember that the members of the Armed Forces give their basic allegiance solely to the United States. Of that fact all of us are certain. But pride of service and mistaken zeal in promoting particular doctrine has more than once occasioned the kind of difficulty of which I have just spoken.

I am not attempting today to pass judgment on the charge of harmful service rivalries. But one thing is sure. Whatever they are, America wants them stopped.

Recently I have had under special study the never-ending problem of efficient organization, complicated as it is by new weapons. Soon my conclusions will be finalized. I shall promptly take such Executive action as is necessary and, in a separate message, I shall present appropriate recommendations to the Congress.

Meanwhile, without anticipating the detailed form that a reorganization should take, I can state its main lines in terms of objectives:

A major purpose of military organization is to achieve real unity in the Defense establishment in all the principal features of military activities. Of all these, one of the most important to our nation's security is strategic planning and control. This work must be done under unified direction.

The defense structure must be one which, as a whole, can assume, with top efficiency and without friction, the defense of America. The Defense establishment must therefore plan for a better integration of its defensive resources, particularly with respect to the newer weapons now building and under development. These obviously require full coordination in their development, production and use. Good organization can help assure this coordination.

In recognition of the need for single control in some of our most advanced development projects, the Secretary of Defense has already decided to concentrate into one organization all the anti-missile and satellite technology undertaken within the Department of Defense.

Another requirement of military organization is a clear subordination of the military services to duly constituted civilian authority. This control must be real; not merely on the surface.

Next there must be assurance that an excessive number of compartments in organization will not create costly and confusing compartments in our scientific and industrial effort.

Finally, to end inter-service disputes requires clear organization and decisive central direction, supported by the unstinted cooperation of every individual in the defense establishment, civilian and military.

2. ACCELERATED DEFENSE EFFORT

The second major action item is the acceleration of the defense effort in particular areas affected by the fast pace of scientific and technological advance.

Some of the points at which improved and increased effort are most essential are these:

We must have sure warning in case of attack. The improvement of warning equipment is becoming increasingly important as we approach the period when long-range missiles will come into use.

We must protect and disperse our striking forces and increase their readiness for instant reaction. This means more base facilities and standby crews.

We must maintain deterrent retaliatory power. This means, among other things, stepped-up long range missile programs; accelerated programs for other effective missile systems; and, for some years, more advanced aircraft.

We must maintain freedom of the seas. This means nuclear submarines and cruisers; improved anti-submarine weapons; missile ships; and the like.

We must maintain all necessary types of mobile forces to deal with local conflicts, should there be need. This means further improvements in equipment, mobility, tactics and fire power.

Through increases in pay and incentive, we must maintain in the armed forces the skilled manpower modern military forces require.

We must be forward-looking in our research and development to anticipate and achieve the unimagined weapons of the future.

With these and other improvements, we intend to assure that our vigilance, power, and technical excellence keep abreast of any realistic threat we face.

3. MUTUAL AID

Third: We must continue to strengthen our mutual security efforts. Most people now realize that our programs of military aid and defense support are an integral part of our own defense effort. If the foundations of the Free World structure were progressively allowed to crumble under the pressure of communist imperialism, the entire house of freedom would be in danger of collapse.

As for the mutual economic assistance program, the benefit to us is threefold. First, the countries receiving this aid become bulwarks against communist encroachment as their military defenses and economies are strengthened. Nations that are conscious of a steady improvement in their industry, education, health and standard of living are not apt to fall prey to the blandishments of communist imperialists.

Second, these countries are helped to reach the point where mutually profitable trade can expand between them and us.

Third, the mutual confidence that comes from working together on constructive projects creates an atmosphere in which real understanding and peace can flourish.

To help bring these multiple benefits, our economic aid effort should be made more effective.

In proposals for future economic aid, I am stressing a greater use of repayable loans, through the Development Loan Fund, through funds generated by sale of surplus farm products, and through the Export-Import Bank.

While some increase in Government funds will be required, it remains our objective to encourage shifting to the use of private capital sources as rapidly as possible.

One great obstacle to the economic aid program in the past has been, not a rational argument against it on the merits, but a catchword: "give-away program."

The real fact is that no investment we make in our own security and peace can pay us greater dividends than necessary amounts of economic aid to friendly nations. This is no "give-away." Let's stick to facts !

We cannot afford to have one of our most essential security programs shot down with a slogan !

4. MUTUAL TRADE

Fourth: Both in our national interest, and in the interest of world peace, we must have a five-year extension of the Trade Agreements Act with broadened authority to negotiate.

World trade supports a significant segment of American industry and agriculture. It provides employment for four and one-half million American workers. It helps supply our ever increasing demand for raw materials. It provides the opportunity for American free enterprise to develop on a worldwide scale. It strengthens our friends and increases their desire to be friends. World trade helps to lay the groundwork for peace by making all free nations of the world stronger and more self-reliant.

America is today the world's greatest trading nation. If we use this great asset wisely to meet the expanding demands of the world, we shall not only provide future opportunities for our own business, agriculture, and labor, but in the process strengthen our security posture and other prospects for a prosperous, harmonious world.

As President McKinley said, as long ago as 1901: "Isolation is no longer possible or desirable .... The period of exclusiveness is past."

5. SCIENTIFIC COOPERATION WITH OUR ALLIES

Fifth: It is of the highest importance that the Congress enact the necessary legislation to enable us to exchange appropriate scientific and technical information with friendly countries as part of our effort to achieve effective scientific cooperation.

It is wasteful in the extreme for friendly allies to consume talent and money in solving problems that their friends have already solved—all because of artificial barriers to sharing. We cannot afford to cut ourselves off from the brilliant talents and minds of scientists in friendly countries. The task ahead will be hard enough without handcuffs of our own making.

The groundwork for this kind of cooperation has already been laid in discussions among NATO countries. Promptness in following through with legislation will be the best possible evidence of American unity of purpose in cooperating with our friends.

6. EDUCATION AND RESEARCH

Sixth: In the area of education and research, I recommend a balanced program to improve our resources, involving an investment of about a billion dollars over a four year period. This involves new activities by the Department of Health, Education and Welfare designed principally to encourage improved teaching quality and student opportunities in the interests of national security. It also provides a five-fold increase in sums available to the National Science Foundation for its special activities in stimulating and improving science education.

Scrupulous attention has been paid to maintaining local control of educational policy, spurring the maximum amount of local effort, and to avoiding undue stress on the physical sciences at the expense of other branches of learning.

In the field of research, I am asking for substantial increases in basic research funds, including a doubling of the funds available to the National Science Foundation for this purpose.

But Federal action can do only a part of the job. In both education and research, redoubled exertions will be necessary on the part of all Americans if we are to rise to the demands of our times. This means hard work on the part of state and local governments, private industry, schools and colleges, private organizations and foundations, teachers, parents, and—perhaps most important of all—the student himself, with his bag of books and his homework.

With this kind of all-inclusive campaign, I have no doubt that we can create the intellectual capital we need for the years ahead, invest it in the right places—and do all this, not as regimented pawns, but as free men and women !

7. SPENDING AND SAVING

Seventh: To provide for this extra effort for security, we must apply stern tests of priority to other expenditures, both military and civilian. This extra effort involves, most immediately, the need for a supplemental defense appropriation of

$1.3 billion for fiscal year 1958.

In the 1959 budget, increased expenditures for missiles, nuclear ships, atomic energy, research and development, science and education, a special contingency fund to deal with possible new technological discoveries, and increases in pay and incentives to obtain and retain competent manpower add up to a total increase over the comparable figures in the 1957 budget of about $4 billion.

I believe that, in spite of these necessary increases, we should strive to finance the 1959 security effort out of expected revenues. While we now believe that expected revenues and expenditures will roughly balance, our real purpose will be to achieve adequate security, but always with the utmost regard for efficiency and careful management.

This purpose will require the cooperation of Congress in making careful analysis of estimates presented, reducing expenditure on less essential military programs and installations, postponing some new civilian programs, transferring some to the states, and curtailing or eliminating others.

Such related matters as the national debt ceiling and tax revenues will be dealt with in later messages.

8. WORKS OF PEACE

My last call for action is not primarily addressed to the Congress and people of the United States. Rather, it is a message from the people of the United States to all other peoples, especially those of the Soviet Union. This is the spirit of what we would like to say:

"In the last analysis, there is only one solution to the grim problems that lie ahead. The world must stop the present plunge toward more and more destructive weapons of war, and turn the corner that will start our steps firmly on the path toward lasting peace.

"Our greatest hope for success lies in a universal fact: the people of the world, as people, have always wanted peace and want peace now.

"The problem, then, is to find a way of translating this universal desire into action. "This will require more than words of peace. It requires works of peace."

Now, may I try to give you some concrete examples of the kind of works of peace that might make a beginning in the new direction.

For a start our people should learn to know each other better. Recent negotiations in Washington have provided a basis in principle for greater freedom of communication and exchange of people. I urge the Soviet government to cooperate in turning principle into practice by prompt and tangible actions that will break down the unnatural barriers that have blocked the flow of thought and understanding between our people.

Another kind of work of peace is cooperation on projects of human welfare. For example, we now have it within our power to eradicate from the face of the earth that age-old scourge of mankind: malaria. We are embarking with other nations in an all-out five-year campaign to blot out this curse forever. We invite the Soviets to join with us in this great work of humanity.

Indeed, we would be willing to pool our efforts with the Soviets in other campaigns against the diseases that are the common enemy of all mortals—such as cancer and heart disease.

If people can get together on such projects, is it not possible that we could then go on to a full-scale cooperative program of Science for Peace?

We have as a guide and inspiration the success of our Atoms-for-Peace proposal, which in only a few years, under United Nations auspices, became a reality in the International Atomic Energy Agency.

A program of Science for Peace might provide a means of funneling into one place the results of research from scientists everywhere and from there making it available to all parts of the world.

There is almost no limit to the human betterment that could result from such cooperation. Hunger and disease could increasingly be driven from the earth. The age-old dream of a good life for all could, at long last, be translated into reality.

But of all the works of peace, none is more needed now than a real first step toward disarmament.

Last August the United Nations General Assembly, by an overwhelming vote, approved a disarmament plan that we and our allies sincerely believed to be fair and practical. The Soviets have rejected both the plan, and the negotiating procedure set up by the United Nations. As a result, negotiation on this supremely important issue is now at a stand-still.

But the world cannot afford to stand still on disarmament! We must never give up the search for a basis of agreement.

Our allies from time to time develop differing ideas on how to proceed. We must concert these convictions among ourselves. Thereafter, any reasonable proposal that holds promise for disarmament and reduction of tension must be heard, discussed, and, if possible, negotiated.

But a disarmament proposal, to hold real promise, must at the minimum have one feature: reliable means to ensure compliance by all. It takes actions and demonstrated integrity on both sides to create and sustain confidence. And confidence in a genuine disarmament agreement is vital, not only to the signers of the agreement, but also to the millions of people all over the world who are weary of tensions and armaments.

I say once more, to all peoples, that we will always go the extra mile with anyone on earth if it will bring us nearer a genuine peace.

CONCLUSION

These, then, are the ways in which we must funnel our energies more efficiently into the task of advancing security and peace.

These actions demand and expect two things of the American people: sacrifice, and a high degree of understanding. For sacrifice to be effective it must be intelligent. Sacrifice must be made for the right purpose and in the right place—even if that place happens to come close to home !

After all, it is no good demanding sacrifice in general terms one day, and the next day, for local reasons, opposing the elimination of some unneeded Federal facility.

It is pointless to condemn Federal spending in general, and the next moment condemn just as strongly an effort to reduce the particular Federal grant that touches one's own interest.

And it makes no sense whatever to spend additional billions on military strength to deter a potential danger, and then, by cutting aid and trade programs, let the world succumb to a present danger in economic guise.

My friends of the Congress: The world is waiting to see how wisely and decisively a free representative government will now act.

I believe that this Congress possesses and will display the wisdom promptly to do its part in translating into law the actions demanded by our nation's interests. But, to make law effective, our kind of government needs the full voluntary support of millions of Americans for these actions.

I am fully confident that the response of the Congress and of the American people will make this time of test a time of honor. Mankind then will see more clearly than ever that the future belongs, not to the concept of the regimented atheistic state, but to the people—the God-fearing, peace-loving people of all the world.

2.7 Dwight D. Eisenhower's Seventh State of the Union Address

Mr. President, Mr. Speaker, Members of the 86th Congress, my fellow citizens: This is the moment when Congress and the Executive annually begin their cooperative work to build a better America.

One basic purpose unites us: To promote strength and security, side by side with liberty and opportunity.

As we meet today, in the 170th year of the Republic, our Nation must continue to provide--as all other free governments have had to do throughout time--a satisfactory answer to a question as old as history. It is: Can Government based upon liberty and the God-given rights of man, permanently endure when ceaselessly challenged by a dictatorship, hostile to our mode of life, and controlling an economic and military power of great and growing strength?

For us the answer has always been found, and is still found in the devotion, the vision, the courage and the fortitude of our people.

Moreover, this challenge we face, not as a single powerful nation, but as one that has in recent decades reached a position of recognized leadership in the Free World.

We have arrived at this position of leadership in an era of remarkable productivity and growth. It is also a time when man's power of mass destruction has reached fearful proportions.

Possession of such capabilities helps create world suspicion and tension. We, on our part, know that we seek only a just peace for all, with aggressive designs against no one. Yet we realize that there is uneasiness in the world because of a belief on the part of peoples that through arrogance, miscalculation or fear of attack, catastrophic war could be launched. Keeping the peace in today's world more than ever calls for the utmost in the nation's resolution, wisdom, steadiness and unremitting effort.

We cannot build peace through desire alone. Moreover, we have learned the bitter lesson that international agreements, historically considered by us as sacred, are regarded in Communist doctrine and in practice to be mere scraps of paper. The most recent proof of their disdain of international obligations, solemnly undertaken, is their announced intention to abandon their responsibilities respecting Berlin.

As a consequence, we can have no confidence in any treaty to which Communists are a party except where such a treaty provides within itself for self-enforcing mechanisms. Indeed, the demonstrated disregard of the Communists of their own pledges is one of the greatest obstacles to success in substituting the Rule of Law for rule by force.

Yet step by step we must strengthen the institutions of peace--a peace that rests upon justice--a peace that depends upon a deep knowledge and dear understanding by all peoples of the cause and consequences of possible failure in this great purpose.

To achieve this peace we seek to prevent war at any place and in any dimension. If, despite our best efforts, a local dispute should flare into armed hostilities, the next problem would be to keep the conflict from spreading, and so compromising freedom. In support of these objectives we maintain forces of great power and flexibility.

Our formidable air striking forces are a powerful deterrent to general war. Large and growing portions of these units can depart from their bases in a matter of minutes. Similar forces are included in our naval fleets.

Ground and other tactical formations can move with swiftness and precision, when requested by friendly and responsible governments, to help curb threatened aggression. The stabilizing influence of this capacity has been dramatically demonstrated more than once over the past year.

Our military and related scientific progress has been highly gratifying.

Great strides have been made in the development of ballistic missiles. Intermediate range missiles are now being deployed in operational units. The Arias intercontinental ballistic missile program has been marked by rapid development as evidenced by recent successful tests. Missile training units have been established and launching sites are far along in construction.

New aircraft that fly at twice the speed of sound are entering our squadrons.

We have successfully placed five satellites in orbit, which have gathered information of scientific importance never before available. Our latest satellite illustrates our steady advance in rocketry and foreshadows new developments in world-wide communications.

Warning systems constantly improve.

Our atomic submarines have shattered endurance records and made historic voyages under the North Polar Sea.

A major segment of our national scientific and engineering community is working intensively to achieve new and greater developments. Advance in military technology requires adequate financing but, of course, even more, it requires talent and time.

All this is given only as a matter of history; as a record of our progress in space and ballistic missile fields in no more than four years of intensive effort. At the same time we clearly recognize that some of the recent Soviet accomplishments in this particular technology are indeed brilliant.

Under the law enacted last year the Department of Defense is being reorganized to give the Secretary of Defense full authority over the military establishment. Greater efficiency, more cohesive effort and speedier reaction to emergencies are among the many advantages we are already noting from these changes.

These few highlights point up our steady military gains. We are rightfully gratified by the achievements they represent. But we must remember that these imposing armaments are purchased at great cost.

National Security programs account for nearly sixty percent of the entire Federal budget for this coming fiscal year. Modern weapons are exceedingly expensive.

The overall cost of introducing ATLAS into our armed forces will average $35 million per missile on the firing line.

This year we are investing an aggregate of close to $7 billion in missile programs alone.

Other billions go for research, development, test and evaluation of new weapons systems.

Our latest atomic submarines will cost $50 millions each, while some special types will cost three times as much.

We are now ordering fighter aircraft which are priced at fifty times as much as the fighters of World War II. We are buying certain bombers that cost their weight in gold.

These sums are tremendous, even when compared with the marvelous resiliency and capacity of our economy.

Such expenditures demand both balance and perspective in our planning for defense. At every turn, we must weigh, judge and select. Needless duplication of weapons and forces must be avoided.

We must guard against feverish building of vast armaments to meet glibly predicted moments of so-called "maximum peril." The threat we face is not sporadic or dated: It is continuous. Hence we must not be swayed in our calculations either by groundless fear or by complacency. We must avoid extremes, for vacillation between extremes is inefficient, costly, and destructive of morale. In these days of unceasing technological advance, we must plan our defense expenditures systematically and with care, fully recognizing that obsolescence compels the never-ending replacement of older weapons with new ones.

The defense budget for the coming year has been planned on the basis of these principles and considerations. Over these many months I have personally participated in its development.

The aim is a sensible posture of defense. The secondary aim is increased efficiency and avoidance of waste. Both are achieved by this budgetary plan.

Working by these guide lines I believe with all my heart that America can be as sure of the strength and efficiency of her armed forces as she is of their loyalty. I am equally sure that the nation will thus avoid useless expenditures which, in the name of security, might tend to undermine the economy and, therefore, the nation's safety.

Our own vast strength is only a part of that required for dependable security. Because of this we have joined with nearly 50 other nations in collective security arrangements. In these common undertakings each nation is expected to contribute what it can in sharing the heavy load. Each supplies part of a strategic deployment to protect the forward boundaries of freedom.

Constantly we seek new ways to make more effective our contribution to this system of collective security. Recently I have asked a Committee of eminent Americans of both parties to re-appraise our military assistance programs and the relative emphasis which should be placed on military and economic aid.

I am hopeful that preliminary recommendations of this Committee will be available in time to assist in shaping the Mutual Security program for the coming fiscal year.

Any survey of the free world's defense structure cannot fail to impart a feeling of regret that so much of our effort and resources must be devoted to armaments. At Geneva and elsewhere we continue to seek technical and other agreements that may help to open up, with some promise, the issues of international disarmament. America will never give up the hope that eventually all nations can, with mutual confidence, drastically reduce these non-productive expenditures.

II.

The material foundation of our national safety is a strong and expanding economy. This we have--and this we must maintain. Only with such an economy can we be secure and simultaneously provide for the well-being of our people.

A year ago the nation was experiencing a decline in employment and output. Today that recession is fading into history, and this without gigantic, hastily-improvised public works projects or untimely tax reductions. A healthy and vigorous recovery has been under way since last May. New homes are being built at the highest rate in several years. Retail sales are at peak levels. Personal income is at an all-time high.

The marked forward thrust of our economy reaffirms our confidence in competitive enterprise. But--clearly--wisdom and prudence in both the public and private sectors of the economy are always necessary.

Our outlook is this: 1960 commitments for our armed forces, the Atomic Energy Commission and Military Assistance exceed 47 billion dollars. In the foreseeable future they are not likely to be significantly lower. With an annual population increase of three million, other governmental costs are bound to mount.

After we have provided wisely for our military strength, we must judge how to allocate our remaining government resources most effectively to promote our well-being and economic growth.

Federal programs that will benefit all citizens are moving forward. Next year we will be spending increased amounts on health programs; on Federal assistance to science and education; on the development of the nation's water resources; on the renewal of urban areas; and on our vast system of Federal-aid highways.

Each of these additional outlays is being made necessary by the surging growth of America.

Let me illustrate. Responsive to this growth, Federal grants and long term loans to assist 14 major types of capital improvements in our cities will total over 2 billion dollars in 1960--double the expenditure of two years ago. The major responsibility for development in these fields rests in the localities, even though the Federal Government will continue to do its proper part in meeting the genuine needs of a burgeoning population.

But the progress of our economy can more than match the growth of our needs. We need only to act wisely and confidently.

Here, I hope you will permit me to digress long enough to express something that is much on my mind.

The basic question facing us today is more than mere survival--the military defense of national life and territory. It is the preservation of a way of life.

We must meet the world challenge and at the same time permit no stagnation in America.

Unless we progress, we regress.

We can successfully sustain security and remain true to our heritage of freedom if we clearly visualize the tasks ahead and set out to perform them with resolution and fervor. We must first define these tasks and then understand what we must do to perform them.

If progress is to be steady we must have long term guides extending far ahead, certainly five, possibly even ten years. They must reflect the knowledge that before the end of five years we will have a population of over 190 million. They must be goals that stand high, and so inspire every citizen to climb always toward mounting levels of moral, intellectual and material strength. Every advance toward them must stir pride in individual and national achievements.

To define these goals, I intend to mobilize help from every available source.

We need more than politically ordained national objectives to challenge the best efforts of free men and women. A group of selfless and devoted individuals, outside of government, could effectively participate in making the necessary appraisal of the potentials of our future. The result would be establishment of national goals that would not only spur us on to our finest efforts, but would meet the stern test of practicality.

The Committee I plan will comprise educators and representatives of labor, management, finance, the professions and every other kind of useful activity.

Such a study would update and supplement, in the light of continuous changes in our society and its economy, the monumental work of the Committee on Recent Social Trends which was appointed in 1931 by President Hoover. Its report has stood the test of time and has had a beneficial influence on national development. The new Committee would be concerned, among other things, with the acceleration of our economy's growth and the living standards of our people, their health and education, their better assurance of life and liberty and their greater opportunities. It would also be concerned with methods to meet such goals and what levels of government--Local, State, or Federal--might or should be particularly concerned.

As one example, consider our schools, operated under the authority of local communities and states. In their capacity and in their quality they conform to no recognizable standards. In some places facilities are ample, in others meager. Pay of teachers ranges between wide limits, from the adequate to the shameful. As would be expected, quality of teaching varies just as widely. But to our teachers we commit the most valuable possession of the nation and of the family--our children.

We must have teachers of competence. To obtain and hold them we need standards. We need a National Goal. Once established I am certain that public opinion would compel steady progress toward its accomplishment.

Such studies would be helpful, I believe, to government at all levels and to all individuals. The goals so established could help us see our current needs in perspective. They will spur progress.

We do not forget, of course, that our nation's progress and fiscal integrity are interdependent and inseparable. We can afford everything we clearly need, but we cannot afford one cent of waste. We must examine every item of governmental expense critically. To do otherwise would betray our nation's future. Thrift is one of the characteristics that has made this nation great. Why should we ignore it now?

We must avoid any contribution to inflationary processes, which could disrupt sound growth in our economy.

Prices have displayed a welcome stability in recent months and, if we are wise and resolute, we will not tolerate inflation in the years to come. But history makes clear the risks inherent in any failure to deal firmly with the .basic causes of inflation. Two of the most important of these causes are the wage-price spiral and continued deficit financing.

Inflation would reduce job opportunities, price us out of world markets, shrink the value of savings and penalize the thrift so essential to finance a growing economy.

Inflation is not a Robin Hood, taking from the rich to give to the poor. Rather, it deals most cruelly with those who can least protect themselves. It strikes hardest those millions of our citizens whose incomes do not quickly rise with the cost of living. When prices soar, the pensioner and the widow see their security undermined, the man of thrift sees his savings melt away; the white collar worker, the minister, and the teacher see their standards of living dragged down.

Inflation can be prevented. But this demands statesmanship on the part of business and labor leaders and of government at all levels.

We must encourage the self-discipline, the restraint necessary to curb the wage-price spiral and we must meet current costs from current revenue.

To minimize the danger of future soaring prices and to keep our economy sound and expanding, I shall present to the Congress certain proposals.

First, I shall submit a balanced budget for the next year, a year expected to be the most prosperous in our history. It is a realistic budget with wholly attainable objectives.

If we cannot live within our means during such a time of rising prosperity, the hope for fiscal integrity will fade. If we persist in living beyond our means, we make it difficult for every family in our land to balance its own household budget. But to live within our means would be a tangible demonstration of the self-discipline needed to assure a stable dollar.

The Constitution entrusts the Executive with many functions, but the Congress--and the Congress alone--has the power of the purse. Ultimately upon Congress rests responsibility for determining the scope and amount of Federal spending.

By working together, the Congress and the Executive can keep a balance between income and outgo. If this is done there is real hope that we can look forward to a time in the foreseeable future when needed tax reforms can be accomplished.

In this hope, I am requesting the Secretary of the Treasury to prepare appropriate proposals for revising, at the proper time, our tax structure, to remove inequities and to enhance incentives for all Americans to work, to save, and to invest. Such recommendations will be made as soon as our fiscal condition permits. These prospects will be brightened if 1960 expenditures do not exceed the levels recommended.

Second, I shall recommend to the Congress that the Chief Executive be given the responsibility either to approve or to veto specific items in appropriations and authorization bills. 1 This would save tax dollars.

[1] At this point the message, as recorded from the floor and printed in the Congressional Record, shows the following interpolation: I assure you gentlemen that I know this recommendation has been made time and again by every President that has appeared in this hall for many years, but I say this, it still is one of the most important corrections that could be made in our annual expenditure program, because this would save tax dollars. [Applause]

Third, to reduce Federal operations in an area where private enterprise can do the job, I shall recommend legislation for greater flexibility in extending Federal credit, and in improving the procedures under which private credits are insured or guaranteed. Present practices have needlessly added large sums to Federal expenditures.

Fourth, action is required to make more effective use of the large Federal expenditures for agriculture and to achieve greater fiscal control in this area.

Outlays of the Department of Agriculture for the current fiscal year for the support of farm prices on a very few farm products will exceed five billion dollars. That is a sum equal to approximately two-fifths of the net income of all farm operators in the entire United States.

By the end of this fiscal year it is estimated that there will be in Government hands surplus farm products worth about nine billion dollars. And by July 1, 1959, Government expenditures for storage, interest, and handling of its agricultural inventory will reach a rate of one billion dollars a year.

This level of expenditure for farm products could be made willingly for a temporary period if it were leading to a sound solution of the problem. But unfortunately this is not true. We need new legislation.

In the past I have sent messages to the Congress requesting greater freedom for our farmers to manage their own farms and greater freedom for markets to reflect the wishes of producers and consumers. Legislative changes that followed were appropriate in direction but did not go far enough.

The situation calls for prompt and forthright action. Recommendation for action will be contained in a message to be transmitted to the Congress shortly.

These fiscal and related actions will help create an environment of price stability for economic growth. However, certain additional measures are needed.

I shall ask Congress to amend the Employment Act of 1946 to make it clear that Government intends to use all appropriate means to protect the buying power of the dollar.

I am establishing a continuing Cabinet group on Price Stability for Economic Growth to study governmental and private policies affecting costs, prices, and economic growth. It will strive also to build a better public understanding of the conditions necessary for maintaining growth and price stability.

Studies are being undertaken to improve our information on prices, wages, and productivity.

I believe all citizens in all walks of life will support this program of action to accelerate economic growth and promote price stability.

III.

I take up next certain aspects of our international situation and our programs to strengthen it.

America's security can be assured only within a world community strong, stable, independent nations, in which the concepts of freedom, justice and human dignity can flourish.

There can be no such thing as Fortress America. If ever we were reduced to the isolation implied by that term, we would occupy a prison, not a fortress. The question whether we can afford to help other nations that want to defend their freedom but cannot fully do so from their own means, has only one answer: we can and we must, we have been doing so since 1947.

Our foreign policy has long been dedicated to building a permanent and just peace.

During the past six years our free world security arrangements have been bolstered and the bonds of freedom have been more closely knit. Our friends in Western Europe are experiencing new internal vitality, and are increasingly more able to resist external threats.

Over the years the world has come to understand clearly that it is our firm policy not to countenance aggression. In Lebanon, Taiwan, and Berlin--our stand has been dear, right, and expressive of the determined will of a united people.

Acting with other free nations we have undertaken the solemn obligation to defend the people of free Berlin against any effort to destroy their freedom. In the meantime we shall constantly seek meaningful agreements to settle this and other problems, knowing full well that not only the integrity of a single city, but the hope of all free peoples is at stake.

We need, likewise, to continue helping to build the economic base so essential to the Free World's stability and strength.

The International Monetary Fund and the World Bank have both fully proven their worth as instruments of international financial cooperation. Their Executive Directors have recommended an increase in each member country's subscription. I am requesting the Congress for immediate approval of our share of these increases.

We are now negotiating with representatives of the twenty Latin American Republics for the creation of an inter-American financial institution. Its purpose would be to join all the American Republics in a common institution which would promote and finance development in Latin America, and make more effective the use of capital from the World Bank, the Export-Import Bank, and private sources.

Private enterprise continues to make major contributions to economic development in all parts of the world. But we have not yet marshalled the full potential of American business for this task, particularly in countries which have recently attained their independence. I shall present to this Congress a program designed to encourage greater participation by private enterprise in economic development abroad.

Further, all of us know that to advance the cause of freedom we must do much more than help build sound economies. The spiritual, intellectual, and physical strength of people throughout the world will in the last analysis determine their willingness and their ability to resist Communism.

To give a single illustration of our many efforts in these fields: We have been a participant in the effort that has been made over the past few years against one of the great scourges of mankind--disease. Through the Mutual Security program public health officials are being trained by American universities to serve in less developed countries. We are engaged in intensive malaria eradication projects in many parts of the world. America's major successes in our own country prove the feasibility of success everywhere.

By these and other means we shall continue and expand our campaign against the afflictions that now bring needless suffering and death to so many of the world's people. We wish to be part of a great shared effort toward the triumph of health.

IV.

America is best described by one word, freedom.

If we hope to strengthen freedom in the world we must be ever mindful of how our own conduct reacts elsewhere. No nation has ever been so floodlighted by world opinion as the United States is today. Everything we do is carefully scrutinized by other peoples throughout the world. The bad is seen along with the good.

Because we are human we err. But as free men we are also responsible for correcting the errors and imperfections of our ways.

Last January I made comprehensive recommendations to the Congress for legislation in the labor-management field. To my disappointment, Congress failed to act. The McClellan Committee disclosures of corruption, racketeering, and abuse of trust and power in labor-management affairs have aroused America and amazed other peoples. They emphasize the need for improved local law enforcement and the enactment of effective Federal legislation to protect the public interest and to insure the rights and economic freedoms of millions of American workers. Halfhearted measures will not do. I shall recommend prompt enactment of legislation designed:

To safeguard workers' funds in union treasuries against misuse of any kind whatsoever.

To protect the rights and freedoms of individual union members, including the basic right to free and secret elections of officers.

To advance true and responsible collective bargaining.

To protect the public and innocent third parties from unfair and coercive practices such as boycotting and blackmail picketing.

The workers and the public must have these vital protections.

In other areas of human rights--freedom from discrimination in voting, in public education, in access to jobs, and in other respects--the world is likewise watching our conduct.

The image of America abroad is not improved when school children, through closing of some of our schools and through no fault of their own, are deprived of their opportunity for an education.

The government of a free people has no purpose more noble than to work for the maximum realization of equality of opportunity under law. This is not the sole responsibility of any one branch of our government. The judicial arm, which has the ultimate authority for interpreting the Constitution, has held that certain state laws and practices discriminate upon racial grounds and are unconstitutional. Whenever the supremacy of the Constitution of the United States is challenged I shall continue to take every action necessary to uphold it.

One of the fundamental concepts of our constitutional system is that it guarantees to every individual, regardless of race, religion, or national origin, the equal protection of the laws. Those of us who are privileged to hold public office have a solemn obligation to make meaningful this inspiring objective. We can fulfill that obligation by our leadership in teaching, persuading, demonstrating, and in enforcing the law.

We are making noticeable progress in the field of civil rights--we are moving forward toward achievement of equality of opportunity for all people everywhere in the United States. In the interest of the nation and of each of its citizens, that progress must continue.

Legislative proposals of the Administration in this field will be submitted to the Congress early in the session. All of us should help to make clear that the government is united in the common purpose of giving support to the law and the decisions of the Courts.

By moving steadily toward the goal of greater freedom under law, for our own people, we shall be the better prepared to work for the cause of freedom under law throughout the world.

All peoples are solely tired of the fear, destruction, and the waste of war. As never before, the world knows the human and material costs of war and seeks to replace force with a genuine role of law among nations.

It is my purpose to intensify efforts during the coming two years in seeking ways to supplement the procedures of the United Nations and other bodies with similar objectives, to the end that the rule of law may replace the rule of force in the affairs of nations. Measures toward this end will be proposed later, including a re-examination of our own relation to the International Court of Justice.

Finally--let us remind ourselves that Marxist scripture is not new; it is not the gospel of the future. Its basic objective is dictatorship, old as history. What is new is the shining prospect that man can build a world where all can live in dignity.

We seek victory--not over any nation or people--but over the ancient enemies of us all; victory over ignorance, poverty, disease, and human degradation wherever they may be found. We march in the noblest of causes--human freedom.

If we make ourselves worthy of America's ideals, if we do not forget that our nation was founded on the premise that all men are creatures of God's making, the world will come to know that it is free men who carry forward the true promise of human progress and dignity.

2.8   Dwight D. Eisenhower's Eighth State of the Union Address

Mr. President, Mr. Speaker, Members of the 86th Congress:

Seven years ago I entered my present office with one long-held resolve overriding all others. I was then, and remain now, determined that the United States shall become an ever more potent resource for the cause of peace--realizing that peace cannot be for ourselves alone, but for peoples everywhere. This determination is shared by the entire Congress--indeed, by all Americans.

My purpose today is to discuss some features of America's position, both at home and in her relations to others.

First, I point out that for us, annual self-examination is made a definite necessity by the fact that we now live in a divided world of uneasy equilibrium, with our side committed to its own protection and against aggression by the other.

With both sides of this divided world in possession of unbelievably destructive weapons, mankind approaches a state where mutual annihilation becomes a possibility. No other fact of today's world equals this in importance--it colors everything we say, plan, and do.

There is demanded of us, vigilance, determination, and the dedication of whatever portion of our resources that will provide adequate security, especially a real deterrent to aggression. These things we are doing.

All these facts emphasize the importance of striving incessantly for a just peace.

Only through the strengthening of the spiritual, intellectual, economic and defensive resources of the Free World can we, in confidence, make progress toward this goal.

Second, we note that recent Soviet deportment and pronouncements suggest the possible opening of a somewhat less strained period in the relationships between the Soviet Union and the Free World. If these Pronouncements be genuine, there is brighter hope of diminishing the intensity of past rivalry and eventually of substituting persuasion for coercion. Whether this is to become an era of lasting promise remains to be tested by actions.

Third, we now stand in the vestibule of a vast new technological age-one that, despite its capacity for human destruction, has an equal capacity to make poverty and human misery obsolete. If our efforts are wisely directed--and if our unremitting efforts for dependable peace begin to attain some success--we can surely become participants in creating an age characterized by justice and rising levels of human well-being.

Over the past year the Soviet Union has expressed an interest in measures to reduce the common peril of war.

While neither we nor any other Free World nation can permit ourselves to be misled by pleasant promises until they are tested by performance, yet we approach this apparently new opportunity with the utmost seriousness. We must strive to break the calamitous cycle of frustrations and crises which, if unchecked, could spiral into nuclear disaster; the ultimate insanity.

Though the need for dependable agreements to assure against resort to force in settling disputes is apparent to both sides yet as in other issues dividing men and nations, we cannot expect sudden and revolutionary results. But we must find some place to begin.

One obvious road on which to make a useful start is in the widening of communication between our two peoples. In this field there are, both sides willing, countless opportunities--most of them well known to us all--for developing mutual understanding, the true foundation of peace.

Another avenue may be through the reopening, on January twelfth, of negotiations looking to a controlled ban on the testing of nuclear weapons. Unfortunately, the closing statement from the Soviet scientists who met with our scientists at Geneva in an unsuccessful effort to develop an agreed basis for a test ban, gives the clear impression that their conclusions have been politically guided. Those of the British and American scientific representatives are their own freely-formed, individual and collective opinion. I am hopeful that as new negotiations begin, truth--not political opportunism--will be the guiding light of the deliberations.

Still another avenue may be found in the field of disarmament, in which the Soviets have professed a readiness to negotiate seriously. They have not, however, made clear the plans they may have, if any, for mutual inspection and verification--the essential condition for any extensive measure of disarmament.

There is one instance where our initiative for peace has recently been successful. A multi-lateral treaty signed last month provides for the exclusively peaceful use of Antarctica, assured by a system of inspection. It provides for free and cooperative scientific research in that continent, and prohibits nuclear explosions there pending general international agreement on the subject. The Treaty is a significant contribution toward peace, international cooperation, and the advancement of science. I shall transmit its text to the Senate for consideration and approval in the near future.

The United States is always ready to participate with the Soviet Union in serious discussion of these or any other subjects that may lead to peace with justice.

Certainly it is not necessary to repeat that the United States has no intention of interfering in the internal affairs of any nation; likewise we reject any attempt to impose its system on us or on other peoples by force or subversion.

This concern for the freedom of other peoples is the intellectual and spiritual cement which has allied us with more than forty other nations in a common defense effort. Not for a moment do we forget that our own fate is firmly fastened to that of these countries; we will not act in any way which would jeopardize our solemn commitments to them.

We and our friends are, of course, concerned with self-defense. Growing out of this concern is the realization that all people of the Free World have a great stake in the progress, in freedom, of the uncommitted and newly emerging nations. These peoples, desperately hoping to lift themselves to decent levels of living must not, by our neglect, be forced to seek help from, and finally become virtual satellites of, those who proclaim their hostility to freedom.

Their natural desire for a better life must not be frustrated by withholding from them necessary technical and investment assistance. This is a problem to be solved not by America alone, but also by every nation cherishing the same ideals and in position to provide help.

In recent years America's partners and friends in Western Europe and Japan have made great economic progress. Their newly found economic strength is eloquent testimony to the striking success of the policies of economic cooperation which we and they have pursued.

The international economy of 1960 is markedly different from that of the early postwar years. No longer is the United States the only major industrial country capable of providing substantial amounts of the resources so urgently needed in the newly-developing countries.

To remain secure and prosperous themselves, wealthy nations must extend the kind of cooperation to the less fortunate members that will inspire hope, confidence and progress. A rich nation can for a time, without noticeable damage to itself, pursue a course of self-indulgence, making its single goal the material ease and comfort of its own citizens-thus repudiating its own spiritual and material stake in a peaceful and prosperous society of nations. But the enmities it will incur, the isolation into which it will descend, and the internal moral and physical softness that will be engendered, will, in the long term, bring it to disaster.

America did not become great through softness and self-indulgence. Her miraculous progress and achievements flow from other qualities far more worthy and substantial--

--adherence to principles and methods consonant with our religious philosophy
--a satisfaction in hard work
--the readiness to sacrifice for worthwhile causes
--the courage to meet every challenge to her progress
--the intellectual honesty and capacity to recognize the true path of her own best interests.

To us and to every nation of the Free World, rich or poor, these qualities are necessary today as never before if we are to march together to greater security, prosperity and peace.

I believe the industrial countries are ready to participate actively in supplementing the efforts of the developing countries to achieve progress.

The immediate need for this kind of cooperation is underscored by the strain in our international balance of payments. Our surplus from foreign business transactions has in recent years fallen substantially short of the expenditures we make abroad to maintain our military establishments overseas, to finance private investment, and to provide assistance to the less developed nations. In 1959 our deficit in balance of payments approached $4 billion.

Continuing deficits of anything like this magnitude would, over time, impair our own economic growth and check the forward progress of the Free World.

We must meet this situation by promoting a rising volume of exports and world trade. Further, we must induce all industrialized nations of the Free World to work together in a new cooperative endeavor to help lift the scourge of poverty from less fortunate nations. This will provide for better sharing of this burden and for still further profitable trade.

New nations, and others struggling with the problems of development, will progress only if they demonstrate faith in their own destiny and possess the will and use their own resources to fulfill it. Moreover, progress in a national transformation can be only gradually earned; there is no easy and quick way to follow from the oxcart to the jet plane. But, just as we drew on Europe for assistance in our earlier years, so now do those new and emerging nations that have this faith and determination deserve help.

Over the last fifteen years, twenty nations have gained political independence. Others are doing so each year. Most of them are woefully lacking in technical capacity and in investment capital; without Free World support in these matters they cannot effectively progress in freedom.

Respecting their need, one of the major focal points of our concern is the South Asian region. Here, in two nations alone, are almost five hundred million people, all working, and working hard, to raise their standards, and in doing so, to make of themselves a strong bulwark against the spread of an ideology that would destroy liberty.

I cannot express to you the depth of my conviction that, in our own and Free World interests, we must cooperate with others to help these people achieve their legitimate ambitions, as expressed in their different multi-year plans. Through the World Bank and other instrumentalities, as well as through individual action by every nation in position to help, we must squarely face this titanic challenge.

All of us must realize, of course, that development in freedom by the newly emerging nations, is no mere matter of obtaining outside financial assistance. An indispensable element in this process is a strong and continuing determination on the part of these nations to exercise the national discipline necessary for any sustained development period. These qualities of determination are particularly essential because of the fact that the process of improvement will necessarily be gradual and laborious rather than revolutionary. Moreover, everyone should be aware that the development process is no short term phenomenon. Many years are required for even the most favorably situated countries.

I shall continue to urge the American people, in the interests of their own security, prosperity and peace, to make sure that their own part of this great project be amply and cheerfully supported. Free World decisions in this matter may spell the difference between world disaster and world progress in freedom.

Other countries, some of which I visited last month, have similar needs.

A common meeting ground is desirable for those nations which are prepared to assist in the development effort. During the past year I have discussed this matter with the leaders of several Western Nations.

Because of its wealth of experience, the Organization for European Economic Cooperation could help with initial studies. The goal is to enlist all available economic resources in the industrialized Free World-especially private investment capital. But I repeat that .this help, no matter how great, can be lastingly effective only if it is used as a supplement to the strength of spirit and will of the people of the newly-developing nations.

By extending this help we hope to make possible the enthusiastic enrollment of these nations under freedom's banner. No more startling contrast to a system of sullen satellites could be imagined.

If we grasp this opportunity to build an age of productive partnership between the less fortunate nations and those that have already achieved a high state of economic advancement, we will make brighter the outlook for a world order based upon security, freedom and peace. Otherwise, the outlook could be dark indeed. We face what may be a turning point in history, and we must act decisively.

As a nation we can successfully pursue these objectives only from a position of broadly based strength.

No matter how earnest is our quest for guaranteed peace, we must maintain a high degree of military effectiveness at the same time we are engaged in negotiating the issue of arms reduction. Until tangible and mutually enforceable arms reduction measures are worked out, we will not weaken the means of defending our institutions.

America possesses an enormous defense power. It is my studied conviction that no nation will ever risk general war against us unless we should be so foolish as to neglect the defense forces we now so powerfully support. It is world-wide knowledge that any nation which might be tempted today to attack the United States, even though our country might sustain great losses, would itself promptly suffer a terrible destruction. But I once again assure all peoples and all nations that the United States, except in defense, will never turn loose this destructive power.

During the past year, our long-range striking power, unmatched today in manned bombers, has taken on new strength as the Atlas intercontinental ballistic missile has entered the operational inventory. In fourteen recent test launchings, at ranges of over 5,000 miles, Atlas has been striking on an average within two miles of the target. This is less than the length of a jet runway--well within the circle of total destruction. Such performance is a great tribute to American scientists and engineers, who in the past five years have had to telescope time and technology to develop these long-range ballistic missiles, where America had none before.

This year, moreover, growing numbers of nuclear-powered submarines will enter our active forces, some to be armed with Polaris missiles. These remarkable ships and weapons, ranging the oceans, will be capable of accurate fire on targets virtually anywhere on earth. Impossible to destroy by surprise attack, they will become one of our most effective sentinels for peace.

To meet situations of less than general nuclear war, we continue to maintain our carrier forces, our many service units abroad, our always ready Army strategic forces and Marine Corps divisions, and the civilian components. The continuing modernization of these forces is a costly but necessary process, and is scheduled to go forward at a rate which will steadily add to our strength.

The deployment of a portion of these forces beyond our shores, on land and sea, is persuasive demonstration of our determination to stand shoulder-to-shoulder with our allies for collective security. Moreover, I have directed that steps be taken to program our military assistance to these allies on a longer range basis. This is necessary for a sounder collective defense system.

Next I refer to our effort in space exploration, which is often mistakenly supposed to be an integral part of defense research and development.

First, America has made great contributions in the past two years to the world's fund of knowledge of astrophysics and space science. These discoveries are of present interest chiefly to the scientific community; but they are important foundation-stones for more extensive exploration of outer space for the ultimate benefit of all mankind.

Second, our military missile program, going forward so successfully, does not suffer from our present lack of very large rocket engines, which are so necessary in distant space exploration. I am assured by experts that the thrust of our present missiles is fully adequate for defense requirements.

Third, the United States is pressing forward in the development of large rocket engines to place much heavier vehicles into space for exploration purposes.

Fourth, in the meantime, it is necessary to remember that we have only begun to probe the environment immediately surrounding the earth. Using launch systems presently available, we are developing satellites to scout the world's weather; satellite relay stations to facilitate and extend communications over the globe; for navigation aids to give accurate bearings to ships and aircraft; and for perfecting instruments to collect and transmit the data we seek. This is the area holding the most promise for early and useful applications of space technology.

Fifth, we have just completed a year's experience with our new space law. I believe it deficient in certain particulars and suggested improvements will be submitted shortly.

The accomplishment of the many tasks I have alluded to requires the continuous strengthening of the spiritual, intellectual, and economic sinews of American life. The steady purpose of our society is to assure justice, before God, for every individual. We must be ever alert that freedom does not wither through the careless amassing of restrictive controls or the lack of courage to deal boldly with the giant issues of the day.

A year ago, when I met with you, the nation was emerging from an economic downturn, even though the signs of resurgent prosperity were not then sufficiently convincing to the doubtful. Today our surging strength is apparent to everyone. 1960 promises to be the most prosperous year in our history.

Yet we continue to be afflicted by nagging disorders.

Among current problems that require solution are:

--the need to protect the public interest in situations of prolonged labor-management stalemate;

--the persistent refusal to come to grips with a critical problem in one sector of American agriculture;

--the continuing threat of inflation, together with the persisting tendency toward fiscal irresponsibility;

--in certain instances the denial to some of our citizens of equal protection of the law.

Every American was disturbed by the prolonged dispute in the steel industry and the protracted delay in reaching a settlement.

We are all relieved that a settlement has at last been achieved in that industry. Percentagewise, by this settlement the increase to the steel companies in employment costs is lower than in any prior wage settlement since World War II. It is also gratifying to note that despite the increase in wages and benefits several of the major steel producers have announced that there will be no increase in steel prices at this time. The national interest demands that in the period of industrial peace which has been assured by the new contract both management and labor make every possible effort to increase efficiency and productivity in the manufacture of steel so that price increases can be avoided.

One of the lessons of this story is that the potential danger to the entire Nation of longer and greater strikes must be met. To insure against such possibilities we must of course depend primarily upon the good commonsense of the responsible individuals. It is my intention to encourage regular discussions between management and labor outside the bargaining table, to consider the interest of the public as well as their mutual interest in the maintenance of industrial peace, price stability and economic growth.

To me, it seems almost absurd for the United States to recognize the need, and so earnestly to seek, for cooperation among the nations unless we can achieve voluntary, dependable, abiding cooperation among the important segments of our own free society.

Failure to face up to basic issues in areas other than those of labor-management can cause serious strains on the firm freedom supports of our society.

I refer to agriculture as one of these areas.

Our basic farm laws were written 27 years ago, in an emergency effort to redress hardship caused by a world-wide depression. They were continued--and their economic distortions intensified--during World War II in order to provide incentives for production of food needed to sustain a war-torn free world.

Today our farm problem is totally different. It is that of effectively adjusting to the changes caused by a scientific revolution. When the original farm laws were written, an hour's farm labor produced only one fourth as much wheat as at present. Farm legislation is woefully out-of-date, ineffective, and expensive.

For years we have gone on with an outmoded system which not only has failed to protect farm income, but also has produced soaring, threatening surpluses. Our farms have been left producing for war while America has long been at peace.

Once again I urge Congress to enact legislation that will gear production more closely to markets, make costly surpluses more manageable, provide greater freedom in farm operations, and steadily achieve increased net farm incomes.

Another issue that we must meet squarely is that of living within our means. This requires restraint in expenditure, constant reassessment of priorities, and the maintenance of stable prices.

We must prevent inflation. Here is an opponent of so many guises that it is sometimes difficult to recognize. But our clear need is to stop continuous and general price rises--a need that all of us can see and feel.

To prevent steadily rising costs and prices calls for stern self-discipline by every citizen. No person, city, state, or organized group can afford to evade the obligation to resist inflation, for every American pays its crippling tax.

Inflation's ravages do not end at the water's edge. Increases in prices of the goods we sell abroad threaten to drive us out of markets that once were securely ours. Whether domestic prices, so high as to be noncompetitive, result from demands for too-high profit margins or from increased labor costs that outrun growth in productivity, the final result is seriously damaging to the nation.

We must fight inflation as we would a fire that imperils our home. Only by so doing can we prevent it from destroying our salaries, savings, pensions and insurance, and from gnawing away the very roots of a free, healthy economy and the nation's security.

One major method by which the Federal government can counter inflation and rising prices is to insure that its expenditures are below its revenues. The debt with which we are now confronted is about 290 billion dollars. With interest charges alone now costing taxpayers about 9 1/2 billions, it is clear that this debt growth must stop. You will be glad to know that despite the unsettling influences of the recent steel strike, we estimate that our accounts will show, on June 30, this year, a favorable balance of approximately $200 million.

I shall present to the Congress for 1961 a balanced budget. In the area of defense, expenditures continue at the record peace-time levels of the last several years. With a single exception, expenditures in every major category of Health,

Education and Welfare will be equal or greater than last year. In Space expenditures the amounts are practically doubled. But the over-all guiding goal of this budget is national need-not response to specific group, local or political insistence.

Expenditure increases, other than those I have indicated, are largely accounted for by the increased cost of legislation previously enacted. 1

[1] At this point the President interpolated the two paragraphs shown in brackets.

[I repeat, this budget will be a balanced one. Expenditures will be 79 billion 8 hundred million. The amount of income over outgo, described in the budget as a Surplus, to be applied against our national debt, is 4 billion 2 hundred million. Personally, I do not feel that any amount can be properly called a "Surplus" as long as the nation is in debt. I prefer to think of such an item as "reduction on our children's inherited mortgage." Once we have established such payments as normal practice, we can profitably make improvements in our tax structure and thereby truly reduce the heavy burdens of taxation.

[In any event, this one reduction will save taxpayers, each ,year, approximately 2 hundred million dollars in interest costs.]

This budget will help ease pressures in our credit and capital markets. It will enhance the confidence of people all over the world in the strength of our economy and our currency and in our individual and collective ability to be fiscally responsible.

In the management of the huge public debt the Treasury is unfortunately not free of artificial barriers. Its ability to deal with the difficult problems in this field has been weakened greatly by the unwillingness of the Congress to remove archaic restrictions. The need for a freer hand in debt management is even more urgent today because the costs of the undesirable financing practices which the Treasury has been forced into are mounting. Removal of this roadblock has high priority in my legislative recommendations.

Still another issue relates to civil rights.

In all our hopes and plans for a better world we all recognize that provincial and racial prejudices must be combatted. In the long perspective of history, the right to vote has been one of the strongest pillars of a free society. Our first duty is to protect this right against all encroachment. In spite of constitutional guarantees, and notwithstanding much progress of recent years, bias still deprives some persons in this country of equal protection of the laws.

Early in your last session I recommended legislation which would help eliminate several practices discriminating against the basic rights of Americans. The Civil Rights Commission has developed additional constructive recommendations. I hope that these will be among the matters to be seriously considered in the current session. I trust that Congress will thus signal to the world that our Government is striving for equality under law for all our people.

Each year and in many ways our nation continues to undergo profound change and growth.

In the past 18 months we have hailed the entry of two more States of the Union--Alaska and Hawaii. We salute these two western stars proudly.

Our vigorous expansion, which we all welcome as a sign of health and vitality, is many-sided. We are, for example, witnessing explosive growth in metropolitan areas.

By 1975 the metropolitan areas of the United States will occupy twice the territory they do today. The roster of urban problems with which they must cope is staggering. They involve water supply, cleaning the air, adjusting local tax systems, providing for essential educational, cultural, and social services, and destroying those conditions which breed delinquency and crime.

In meeting these, we must, if we value our historic freedoms, keep within the traditional framework of our Federal system with powers divided between the national and state governments. The uniqueness of this system may confound the casual observer, but it has worked effectively for nearly 200 years.

I do not doubt that our urban and other perplexing problems can be solved in the traditional American method. In doing so we must realize that nothing is really solved and ruinous tendencies are set in motion by yielding to the deceptive bait of the "easy" Federal tax dollar.

Our educational system provides a ready example. All recognize the vital necessity of having modern school plants, well-qualified and adequately compensated teachers, and of using the best possible teaching techniques and curricula.

We cannot be complacent about educating our youth.

But the route to better trained minds is not through the swift administration of a Federal hypodermic or sustained financial transfusion. The educational process, essentially a local and personal responsibility, cannot be made to leap ahead by crash, centralized governmental action.

The Administration has proposed a carefully reasoned program for helping eliminate current deficiencies. It is designed to stimulate classroom construction, not by substitution of Federal dollars for state and local funds, but by incentives to extend and encourage state and local efforts. This approach rejects the notion of Federal domination or control. It is workable, and should appeal to every American interested in advancement of our educational system in the traditional American way. I urge the Congress to take action upon it.

There is one other subject concerning which I renew a recommendation I made in my State of the Union Message last January. I then advised the Congress of my purpose to intensify our efforts to replace force with a rule of law among nations. From many discussions abroad, I am convinced that purpose is widely and deeply shared by other peoples and nations of the world.

In the same Message I stated that our efforts would include a reexamination of our own relation to the International Court of Justice. The Court was established by the United Nations to decide international legal disputes between nations. In 1946 we accepted the Court's jurisdiction, but subject to a reservation of the right to determine unilaterally whether a matter lies essentially within domestic jurisdiction. There is pending before the Senate, a Resolution which would repeal our present self-judging reservation. I support that Resolution and urge its prompt passage. If this is done, I intend to urge similar acceptance of the Court's jurisdiction by every member of the United Nations.

Here perhaps it is not amiss for me to say to the Members of the Congress, in this my final year of office, a word about the institutions we respectively represent and the meaning which the relationships between our two branches has for the days ahead.

I am not unique as a President in having worked with a Congress controlled by the opposition party--except that no other President ever did it for quite so long! Yet in both personal and official relationships we have weathered the storms of the past five years. For this I am grateful.

My deep concern in the next twelve months, before my successor takes office, is with our joint Congressional-Executive duty to our own and to other nations. Acting upon the beliefs I have expressed here today, I shall devote my full energies to the tasks at hand, whether these involve travel for promoting greater world understanding, negotiations to reduce international discord, or constant discussions and communications with the Congress and the American people on issues both domestic and foreign.

In pursuit of these objectives, I look forward to, and shall dedicate myself to, a close and constructive association with the Congress.

Every minute spent in irrelevant interbranch wrangling is precious time taken from the intelligent initiation and adoption of coherent policies for our national survival and progress.

We seek a common goal--brighter opportunity for our own citizens and a world peace with justice for all.

Before us and our friends is the challenge of an ideology which, for more than four decades, has trumpeted abroad its purpose of gaining ultimate victory over all forms of government at variance with its own.

We realize that however much we repudiate the tenets of imperialistic Communism, it represents a gigantic enterprise grimly pursued by leaders who compel its subjects to subordinate their freedom of action and spirit and personal desires for some hoped-for advantage in the future.

The Communists can present an array of material accomplishments over the past fifteen years that lends a false persuasiveness to many of their glittering promises to the uncommitted peoples.

The competition they provide is formidable.

But in our scale of values we place freedom first--our whole national existence and development have been geared to that basic concept and are responsible for the position of free world leadership to which we have succeeded. It is the highest prize that any nation can possess; it is one that Communism can never offer. And America's record of material accomplishment in freedom is written not only in the unparalleled prosperity of our own nation, but in the many billions we have devoted to the reconstruction of Free World economics wrecked by World War II and in the effective help of many more billions we have given in saving the independence of many others threatened by outside domination. Assuredly we have the capacity for handling the problems in the new era of the world's history we are now entering.

But we must use that capacity intelligently and tirelessly, regardless of personal sacrifice.

The fissure that divides our political planet is deep and wide.

We live, moreover, in a sea of semantic disorder in which old labels no longer faithfully describe.

Police states are called "people's democracies."

Armed conquest of free people is called "liberation."

Such slippery slogans make more difficult the problem of communicating true faith, facts and beliefs.

We must make clear our peaceful intentions, our aspirations for a better world. So doing, we must use language to enlighten the mind, not as the instrument of the studied innuendo and distorter of truth.

And we must live by what we say.

On my recent visit to distant lands I found one statesman after another eager to tell me of the elements of their government that had been borrowed from our American Constitution, and from the indestructible ideals set forth in our Declaration of Independence.

As a nation we take pride that our own constitutional system, and the ideals which sustain it, have been long viewed as a fountainhead of freedom.

By our every action we must strive to make ourselves worthy of this trust, ever mindful that an accumulation of seemingly minor encroachments upon freedom gradually could break down the entire fabric of a free society.

So persuaded, we shall get on with the task before us.

So dedicated, and with faith in the Almighty, humanity shall one day achieve the unity in freedom to which all men have aspired from the dawn of time.

2.9   Dwight D. Eisenhower's Ninth State of the Union Address

To the Congress of the United States:

Once again it is my Constitutional duty to assess the state of the Union.

On each such previous occasion during these past eight years I have outlined a forward course designed to achieve our mutual objective--a better America in a world of peace. This time my function is different.

The American people, in free election, have selected new leadership which soon will be entrusted with the management of our government. A new President shortly will lay before you his proposals to shape the future of our great land. To him, every citizen, whatever his political beliefs, prayerfully extends best wishes for good health and for wisdom and success in coping with the problems that confront our Nation.

For my part, I should like, first, to express to you of the Congress, my appreciation of your devotion to the common good and your friendship over these difficult years. I will carry with me pleasant memories of this association in endeavors profoundly significant to all our people.

We have been through a lengthy period in which the control over the executive and legislative branches of government has been divided between our two great political parties. Differences, of course, we have had, particularly in domestic affairs. But in a united determination to keep this Nation strong and free and to utilize our vast resources for the advancement of all mankind, we have carried America to unprecedented heights.

For this cooperative achievement I thank the American people and those in the Congress of both parties who have supported programs in the interest of our country.

I should also like to give special thanks for the devoted service of my associates in the Executive Branch and the hundreds of thousands of career employees who have implemented our diverse government programs.

My second purpose is to review briefly the record of these past eight years in the hope that, out of the sum of these experiences, lessons will emerge that are useful to our Nation. Supporting this review are detailed reports from the several agencies and departments, all of which are now or will shortly be available to the Congress.

Throughout the world the years since 1953 have been a period of profound change. The human problems in the world grow more acute hour by hour; yet new gains in science and technology continually extend the promise of a better life. People yearn to be free, to govern themselves; yet a third of the people of the world have no freedom, do not govern themselves. The world recognizes the catastrophic nature of nuclear war; yet it sees the wondrous potential of nuclear peace.

During the period, the United States has forged ahead under a constructive foreign policy. The continuing goal is peace, liberty, and well-being--for others as well as ourselves. The aspirations of all peoples are one--peace with justice in freedom. Peace can only be attained collectively as peoples everywhere unite in their determination that liberty and well-being come to all mankind.

Yet while we have worked to advance national aspirations for freedom, a divisive force has been at work to divert that aspiration into dangerous channels. The Communist movement throughout the world exploits the natural striving of all to be free and attempts to subjugate men rather than free them. These activities have caused and are continuing to cause grave troubles in the world.

Here at home these have been times for careful adjustment of our economy from the artificial impetus of a hot war to constructive growth in a precarious peace. While building a new economic vitality without inflation, we have also increased public expenditures to keep abreast of the needs of a growing population and its attendant new problems, as well as our added international responsibilities. We have worked toward these ends in a context of shared responsibility--conscious of the need for maximum scope to private effort and for State and local, as well as Federal, governmental action.

Success in designing and executing national purposes, domestically and abroad, can only come from a steadfast resolution that integrity in the operation of government and in our relations with each other be fully maintained. Only in this way could our spiritual goals be fully advanced.

FOREIGN POLICY

On January 20, 1953, when I took office, the United States was at war. Since the signing of the Korean Armistice in 1953, Americans have lived in peace in highly troubled times.

During the 1956 Suez crisis, the United States government strongly supported United Nations' action--resulting in the ending of the hostilities in Egypt.

Again in 1958, peace was preserved in the Middle East despite new discord. Our government responded to the request of the friendly Lebanese Government for military help, and promptly withdrew American forces as soon as the situation was stabilized.

In 1958 our support of the Republic of China during the all-out bombardment of Quemoy restrained the Communist Chinese from attempting to invade the off-shore islands.

Although, unhappily, Communist penetration of Cuba is real and poses a serious threat, Communist dominated regimes have been deposed in Guatemala and Iran. The occupation of Austria has ended and the Trieste question has been settled.

Despite constant threats to its integrity, West Berlin has remained free.

Important advances have been made in building mutual security arrangements--which lie at the heart of our hopes for future peace and security in the world. The Southeast Asia Treaty Organization has been established; the NATO alliance has been militarily strengthened; the Organization of American States has been further developed as an instrument of inter-American cooperation; the Anzus treaty has strengthened ties with Australia and New Zealand, and a mutual security treaty with Japan has been signed. In addition, the CENTO pact has been concluded, and while we are not officially a member of this alliance we have participated closely in its deliberations.

The "Atoms for Peace" proposal to the United Nations led to the creation of the International Atomic Energy Agency. Our policy has been to push for enforceable programs of inspection against surprise attack, suspension of nuclear testing, arms reduction, and peaceful use of outer space.

The United Nations has been vigorously supported in all of its actions, including the condemnations of the wholesale murder of the people of Tibet by the Chinese Communists and the brutal Soviet repression of the people of Hungary, as well as the more recent UN actions in the Congo.

The United States took the initiative in negotiating the significant treaty to guarantee the peaceful use of vast Antarctica.

The United States Information Agency has been transformed into a greatly improved medium for explaining our policies and actions to audiences overseas, answering the lies of communist propaganda, and projecting a clearer image of American life and culture.

Cultural, technological and educational exchanges with the Soviet Union have been encouraged, and a comprehensive agreement was made which authorized, among other things, the distribution of our Russian language magazine Amerika and the highly successful American Exhibition in Moscow.

This country has continued to withhold recognition of Communist China and to oppose vigorously the admission of this belligerent and unrepentant nation into the United Nations. Red China has yet to demonstrate that it deserves to be considered a "peace-loving" nation.

With communist imperialism held in check, constructive actions were undertaken to strengthen the economies of free world nations. The United States government has given sturdy support to the economic and technical assistance activities of the UN. This country stimulated a doubling of the capital of the World Bank and a 50 percent capital increase in the International Monetary Fund. The Development Loan Fund and the International Development Association were established. The United States also took the lead in creating the Inter-American Development Bank.

Vice President Nixon, Secretaries of State Dulles and Herter and I travelled extensively through the world for the purpose of strengthening the cause of peace, freedom, and international understanding. So rewarding were these visits that their very success became a significant factor in causing the Soviet Union to wreck the planned Summit Conference of 1960.

These vital programs must go on. New tactics will have to be developed, of course, to meet new situations, but the underlying principles should be constant. Our great moral and material commitments to collective security, deterrence of force, international law, negotiations that lead to self-enforcing agreements, and the economic interdependence of free nations should remain the cornerstone of a foreign policy that will ultimately bring permanent peace with justice in freedom to all mankind. The continuing need of all free nations today is for each to recognize clearly the essentiality of an unbreakable bond among themselves based upon a complete dedication to the principles of collective security, effective cooperation and peace with justice.

NATIONAL DEFENSE

For the first time in our nation's history we have consistently maintained in peacetime, military forces of a magnitude sufficient to deter and if need be to destroy predatory forces in the world.

Tremendous advances in strategic weapons systems have been made in the past eight years. Not until 1953 were expenditures on long-range ballistic missile programs even as much as a million dollars a year; today we spend ten times as much each day on these programs as was spent in all of 1952.

No guided ballistic missiles were operational at the beginning of 1953. Today many types give our armed forces unprecedented effectiveness. The explosive power of our weapons systems for all purposes is almost inconceivable.

Today the United States has operational ATLAS missiles which can strike a target 5000 miles away in a half-hour. The POLARIS weapons system became operational last fall and the TITAN is scheduled to become so this year. Next year, more than a year ahead of schedule, a vastly improved ICBM, the solid propellant MINUTEMAN, is expected to be ready.

Squadrons of accurate Intermediate Range Ballistic Missiles are now operational. The THOR and JUPITER IRBMs based in forward areas can hit targets 1500 miles away in 18 minutes.

Aircraft which fly at speeds faster than sound were still in a developmental stage eight years ago. Today American fighting planes go twice the speed of sound. And either our B-58 Medium Range Jet Bomber or our B-52 Long Range Jet Bomber can carry more explosive power than was used by all combatants in World War II--Allies and Axis combined.

Eight years ago we had no nuclear-powered ships. Today 49 nuclear warships have been authorized. Of these, 14 have been commissioned, including three of the revolutionary POLARIS submarines. Our nuclear submarines have cruised under the North Pole and circumnavigated the earth while submerged. Sea warfare has been revolutionized, and the United States is far and away the leader.

Our tactical air units overseas and our aircraft carriers are alert; Army units, guarding the frontiers of freedom in Europe and the Far East, are in the highest state of readiness in peacetime history; our Marines, a third of whom are deployed in the Far East, are constantly prepared for action; our Reserve establishment has maintained high standards of proficiency, and the Ready Reserve now numbers over 2 S million citizen-soldiers.

The Department of Defense, a young and still evolving organization, has twice been improved and the line of command has been shortened in order to meet the demands of modern warfare. These major reorganizations have provided a more effective structure for unified planning and direction of the vast defense establishment. Gradual improvements in its structure and procedures are to be expected.

United States civil defense and nonmilitary defense capacity has been greatly strengthened and these activities have been consolidated in one Federal agency.

The defense forces of our Allies now number five million men, several thousand combatant ships, and over 25,000 aircraft. Programs to strengthen these allies have been consistently supported by the Administration. U.S. military assistance goes almost exclusively to friendly nations on the rim of the communist world. This American contribution to nations who have the will to defend their freedom, but insufficient means, should be vigorously continued. Combined with our Allies, the free world now has a far stronger shield than we could provide alone.

Since 1953, our defense policy has been based on the assumption that the international situation would require heavy defense expenditures for an indefinite period to come, probably for years. In this protracted struggle, good management dictates that we resist overspending as resolutely as we oppose under-spending. Every dollar uselessly spent on military mechanisms decreases our total strength and, therefore, our security. We must not return to the "crash-program" psychology of the past when each new feint by the Communists was responded to in panic. The "bomber gap" of several years ago was always a fiction, and the "missile gap" shows every sign of being the same.

The nation can ill afford to abandon a national policy which provides for a fully adequate and steady level of effort, designed for the long pull; a fast adjustment to new scientific and technological advances; a balanced force of such strength as to deter general war, to effectively meet local situations and to retaliate to attack and destroy the attacker; and a strengthened system of free world collective security.

THE ECONOMY

The expanding American economy passed the half-trillion dollar mark in gross national product early in 1960. The Nation's output of goods and services is now nearly 25 percent higher than in 1952.

In 1959, the average American family had an income of $6,520, 15 percent higher in dollars of constant buying power than in 1952, and the real wages of American factory workers have risen 20 percent during the past eight years. These facts reflect the rising standard of individual and family well-being enjoyed by Americans.

Our Nation benefits also from a remarkable improvement in general industrial peace through strengthened processes of free collective bargaining. Time lost since 1952 because of strikes has been half that lost in the eight years prior to that date. Legislation now requires that union members have the opportunity for full participation in the affairs of their unions. The Administration supported the Landrum-Griffin Act, which I believe is greatly helpful to the vast bulk of American Labor and its leaders, and also is a major step in getting racketeers and gangsters out of labor-management affairs.

The economic security of working men and women has been strengthened by an extension of unemployment insurance coverage to 2.5 million ex-servicemen, 2.4 million Federal employees, and 1.2 million employees of small businesses, and by a strengthening of the Railroad Unemployment Insurance Act. States have been encouraged to improve their unemployment compensation benefits, so that today average weekly benefits are 40 percent higher than in 1953.

Determined efforts have improved workers' safety standards. Enforceable safety standards have been established for longshoremen and ship repair workers; Federal Safety Councils have been increased from 14 to over 100; safety awards have been initiated, and a national construction safety program has been developed.

A major factor in strengthening our competitive enterprise system, and promoting economic growth, has been the vigorous enforcement of antitrust laws over the last eight years and a continuing effort to reduce artificial restraints on competition and trade and enhance our economic liberties. This purpose was also significantly advanced in 1953 when, as one of the first acts of this Administration, restrictive wage and price controls were ended.

An additional measure to strengthen the American system of competitive enterprise was the creation of the Small Business Administration in 1953 to assist existing small businesses and encourage new ones. This agency has approved over $1 billion in loans, initiated a new program to provide long-term capital for small businesses, aided in setting aside $3S billion in government contracts for award to small business concerns, and brought to the attention of individual businessmen, through programs of information and education, new developments in management and production techniques. Since 1952, important tax revisions have been made to encourage small businesses.

Many major improvements in the Nation's transportation system have been made:

--After long years of debate, the dream of a great St. Lawrence Seaway, opening the heartland of America to ocean commerce, has been fulfilled.

--The new Federal Aviation Agency is fostering greater safety in air travel.

--The largest public construction program in history--the 41,000 mile national system of Interstate and Defense highways--has been pushed rapidly forward. Twenty-five percent of this system is now open to traffic.

Efforts to help every American build a better life have included also a vigorous program for expanding our trade with other nations. A 4-year renewal of the Reciprocal Trade Agreements Act was passed in 1958, and a continuing and rewarding effort has been made to persuade other countries to remove restrictions against our exports. A new export expansion program was launched in 1960, inaugurating improvement of export credit insurance and broadening research and information programs to awaken Americans to business opportunities overseas. These actions and generally prosperous conditions abroad have helped push America's export trade to a level of $20 billion in 1960.

Although intermittent declines in economic activity persist as a problem in our enterprise system, recent downturns have been moderate and of short duration. There is, however, little room for complacency. Currently our economy is operating at high levels, but unemployment rates are higher than any of us would like, and chronic pockets of high unemployment persist. Clearly, continued sound and broadly shared economic growth remains a major national objective toward which we must strive through joint private and public efforts.

If government continues to work to assure every American the fullest opportunity to develop and utilize his ability and talent, it will be performing one of its most vital functions, that of advancing the welfare and protecting the dignity, rights, and freedom of all Americans.

GOVERNMENT FINANCE AND ADMINISTRATION

In January 1953, the consumer's dollar was worth only 52 cents in terms of the food, clothing, shelter and other items it would buy compared to 1939. Today, the inflationary spiral which had raised the cost of living by 36 percent between 1946 and 1952 has all but ceased and the value of the dollar virtually stabilized.

In 1954 we had the largest tax cut in history, amounting to $7.4 billion annually, of which over 62 percent went to individuals mostly in the small income brackets.

This Administration has directed constant efforts toward fiscal responsibility. Balanced budgets have been sought when the economy was advancing, and a rigorous evaluation of spending programs has been maintained at all times. Resort to deficit financing in prosperous times could easily erode international confidence in the dollar and contribute to inflation at home. In this belief, I shall submit a balanced budget for fiscal 1962 to the Congress next week.

There has been a firm policy of reducing government competition with private enterprise. This has resulted in the discontinuance of some 2,000 commercial industrial installations and in addition the curtailment of approximately 550 industrial installations operated directly by government agencies.

Also an aggressive surplus disposal program has been carried on to Identify and dispose of unneeded government-owned real property. This has resulted in the addition of a substantial number of valuable properties to local tax rolls, and a significant monetary return to the government.

Earnest and persistent attempts have been made to strengthen the position of State and local governments and thereby to stop the dangerous drift toward centralization of governmental power in Washington.

Significant strides have been made in increasing the effectiveness of government. Important new agencies have been established, such as the Department of Health, Education, and Welfare, the Federal Aviation Agency, and the National Aeronautics and Space Administration. The Council of Economic Advisers was reconstituted.

The operation of our postal system has been modernized to get better and more efficient service. Modernized handling of local mail now brings next-day delivery to 168 million people in our population centers, expanded carrier service now accommodates 9.3 million families in the growing suburbs, and 1.4 million families have been added to the rural delivery service. Common sense dictates that the Postal Service should be on a self-financing basis.

The concept of a trained and dedicated government career service has been strengthened by the provision of life and health insurance benefits, a vastly improved retirement system, a new merit promotion program, and the first effective incentive awards program. With no sacrifice in efficiency, Federal civilian employment since 1953 has been reduced by over a quarter of a million persons.

I am deeply gratified that it was under the urging of this Administration that Alaska and Hawaii became our 49th and 50th States.

AGRICULTURE

Despite the difficulties of administering Congressional programs which apply outmoded prescriptions and which aggravate rather than solve problems, the past eight years brought notable advances in agriculture.

Total agricultural assets are approximately $200 billion--up $36 billion in eight years.

Farm owner equities are at the near record high of $174 billion.

Farm ownership is at a record high with fewer farmers in a tenant and sharecropper status than at any time in our nation's history.

The "Food-for-Peace" program has demonstrated how surplus of American food and fiber can be effectively used to feed and clothe the needy abroad. Aided by this humanitarian program, total agricultural exports have grown from $2.8 billion in 1953 to an average of about $4 billion annually for the past three years. For 1960, exports are estimated at $4.5 billion, the highest volume on record. Under the Food-for-Peace program, the largest wheat transaction in history was consummated with India in 1960.

The problems of low-income farm families received systematic attention for the first time in the Rural Development Program. This program has gone forward in 39 States, yielding higher incomes and a better living for rural people most in need.

The Rural Electrification Administration has helped meet the growing demand for power and telephones in agricultural areas. Ninety-seven percent of all farms now have central station electric power. Dependence upon Federal financing should no longer be necessary.

The Farm Credit Administration has been made an independent agency more responsive to the farmer's needs.

The search for new uses for our farm abundance and to develop new crops for current needs has made major progress. Agricultural research appropriations have increased by 171 percent since 1953.

Farmers are being saved approximately $80 million a year by the repeal in 1956 of Federal taxes on gasoline used in tractors and other machinery.

Since 1953, appropriations have been doubled for county agents, home agents and the Extension Service.

Eligibility for Social Security benefits has been extended to farmers and their families.

Yet in certain aspects our agricultural surplus situation is increasingly grave. For example, our wheat stocks now total 1.3 billion bushels. If we did not harvest one bushel of wheat in this coming year, we would still have all we could eat, all we could sell abroad, all we could give away, and still have a substantial carryover. Extraordinary costs are involved just in management and disposal of this burdensome surplus. Obviously important adjustments must still come. Congress must enact additional legislation to permit wheat and other farm commodities to move into regular marketing channels in an orderly manner and at the same time afford the needed price protection to the farmer. Only then will agriculture again be

78 CHAPTER 2. STATE OF THE UNION ADDRESSES

free, sound, and profitable.

NATURAL RESOURCES

New emphasis has been placed on the care of our national parks. A ten year development program of our National Park System--Mission 66--was initiated and 633,000 acres of park land have been added since 1953.

Appropriations for fish and wildlife operations have more than doubled. Thirty-five new refuges, containing 11,342,000 acres, have been added to the national wildlife management system.

Our Nation's forests have been improved at the most rapid rate in history.

The largest sustained effort in water resources development in our history has taken place. In the field of reclamation alone, over 50 new projects, or project units, have been authorized since 1953--including the billion dollar Colorado River Storage Project. When all these projects have been completed they will have a storage capacity of nearly 43 million acre-feet--an increase of 50 percent over the Bureau of Reclamation's storage capacity in mid-1953. In addition, since 1953 over 450 new navigation flood control and multiple purpose projects of the Corps of Engineers have been started, costing nearly 6 billion dollars.

Soil and water conservation has been advanced as never before. One hundred forty-one projects are now being constructed under the Watershed Protection Program.

Hydroelectric power has been impressively developed through a policy which recognizes that the job to be done requires comprehensive development by Federal, State, and local governments and private enterprise. Teamwork is essential to achieve this objective.

The Federal Columbia River power system has grown from two multipurpose dams with a 2.6 million kilowatt capacity to 17 multipurpose projects completed or under construction with an ultimate installed capacity of 8.1 million kilowatts. After years of negotiation, a Columbia River Storage Development agreement with Canada now opens the way for early realization of unparalleled power, flood control and resource conservation benefits for the Pacific Northwest. A treaty implementing this agreement will shortly be submitted to the Senate.

A farsighted and highly successful program for meeting urgent water needs is being carded out by converting salt water to fresh water. A 75 percent reduction in the cost of this process has already been realized.

Continuous resource development is essential for our expanding economy. We must continue vigorous, combined Federal, State and private programs, at the same time preserving to the maximum extent possible our natural and scenic heritage for future generations.

EDUCATION, SCIENCE, AND TECHNOLOGY

The National Defense Education Act of 1958 is already a milestone in the history of American education. It provides broad opportunities for the intellectual development of all children by strengthening courses of study in science, mathematics, and foreign languages, by developing new graduate programs to train additional teachers, and by providing loans for young people who need financial help to go to college.

The Administration proposed on numerous occasions a broad new five-year program of Federal aid to help overcome the classroom shortage in public elementary and secondary schools. Recommendations were also made to give assistance to colleges and universities for the construction of academic and residential buildings to meet future enrollment increases.

This Administration greatly expanded Federal loans for building dormitories for students, teachers, and nurses training, a program assisting in the construction of approximately 200,000 living accommodations during the past 8 years.

There has been a vigorous acceleration of health, resource and education programs designed to advance the role of the American Indian in our society. Last fall, for example, 91 percent of the Indian children between the ages of 6 and 18 on reservations were enrolled in school. This is a rise of 12 percent since 1953.

In the field of science and technology, startling strides have been made by the new National Aeronautics and Space Administration. In little more than two years, NASA has successfully launched meteorological satellites, such as Tiros I and Tiros II, that promise to revolutionize methods of weather forecasting; demonstrated the feasibility of satellites for global communications by the successful launching of Echo I; produced an enormous amount of valuable scientific data, such as the discovery of the Van Allen Radiation Belt; successfully launched deep-space probes that maintained communication over the greatest range man has ever tracked; and made real progress toward the goal of manned space flights.

These achievements unquestionably make us preeminent today in space exploration for the betterment of mankind. I believe the present organizational arrangements in this area, with the revisions proposed last year, are completely adequate for the tasks ahead.

Americans can look forward to new achievements in space exploration. The near future will hold such wonders as the orbital flight of an astronaut, the landing of instruments on the moon, the launching of the powerful giant Saturn rocket vehicles, and the reconnaissance of Mars and Venus by unmanned vehicles.

The application of atomic energy to industry, agriculture, and medicine has progressed from hope and experiment to reality. American industry and agriculture are making increasing use of radioisotopes to improve manufacturing, testing, and crop-raising. Atomic energy has improved the ability of the healing professions to combat disease, and holds promise for an eventual increase in man's life span.

Education, science, technology and balanced programs of every kind-these are the roadways to progress. With appropriate Federal support, the States and localities can assure opportunities for achieving excellence at all levels of the educational system; and with the Federal government continuing to give wholehearted support to basic scientific research and technology, we can expect to maintain our position of leadership in the world.

CIVIL RIGHTS

The first consequential Federal Civil Rights legislation in 85 years was enacted by Congress on recommendation of the Administration in 1957 and 1960.

A new Civil Rights Division in the Department of Justice has already moved to enforce constitutional rights in such areas as voting and the elimination of Jim Crow laws.

Greater equality of job opportunity in Federal employment and employment with Federal contractors has been effectively provided through the President's Committees on Government Contracts and Government Employment Practices.

The Civil Rights Commission has undertaken important surveys in the fields of housing, voting, and education.

Segregation has been abolished in the Armed Forces, in Veterans' Hospitals, in all Federal employment, and throughout the District of Columbia--administratively accomplished progress in this field that is unmatched in America's recent history.

This pioneering work in civil rights must go on. Not only because discrimination is morally wrong, but also because its impact is more than national--it is world-wide.

HEALTH AND WELFARE

Federal medical research expenditures have increased more than fourfold since 1954.

A vast variety of the approaches known to medical science has been explored to find better methods of treatment and prevention of major diseases, particularly heart diseases, cancer, and mental illness.

The control of air and water pollution has been greatly strengthened.

Americans now have greater protection against harmful, unclean, or misrepresented foods, drugs, or cosmetics through a strengthened Food and Drug Administration and by new legislation which requires that food additives be proved safe for human consumption before use.

A newly established Federal Radiation Council, along with the Department of Health, Education, and Welfare, analyzes and coordinates information regarding radiological activities which affect the public health.

Medical manpower has been increased by Federal grants for teaching and research.

Construction of new medical facilities has been stepped up and extended to include nursing homes, diagnostic and treatment centers, and rehabilitation facilities.

The vocational rehabilitation program has been significantly expanded. About 90,000 handicapped people are now being rehabilitated annually so they are again able to earn their own living with self-respect and dignity.

New legislation provides for better medical care for the needy aged, including those older persons, who, while otherwise self-sufficient, need help in meeting their health care costs. The Administration recommended a major expansion of this effort.

The coverage of the Social Security Act has been broadened since 1953 to make 11 million additional people eligible for retirement, disability or survivor benefits for themselves or their dependents, and the Social Security benefits have been substantially improved.

Grants to the States for maternal and child welfare services have been increased.

The States, aided by Federal grants, now assist some 6 million needy people through the programs of Old Age Assistance, Aid to Dependent Children, Aid to the Blind, and Aid to the Totally and Permanently Disabled.

HOUSING AND URBAN DEVELOPMENT

More houses have been built during the past eight years--over nine million--than during any previous eight years in history.

An historic new approach--Urban Renewal--now replaces piecemeal thrusts at slum pockets and urban blight. Communities engaged in urban renewal have doubled and renewal projects have more than tripled since 1953. An estimated 68 projects in 50 cities will be completed by the end of the current fiscal year; another 577 projects will be underway, and planning for 310 more will be in process. A total of $2 billion in Federal grants will ultimately be required to finance these 955 projects.

New programs have been initiated to provide more and better housing for elderly people. Approximately 25,000 units especially designed for the elderly have been built, started, or approved in the past three years.

For the first time, because of Federal help and .encouragement, 90 metropolitan areas and urban regions and 1140 smaller towns throughout the country are making comprehensive development plans for their future growth and development.

American communities have been helped to plan water and sanitation systems and schools through planning advances for 1600 public works projects with a construction cost of nearly $2 billion.

Mortgage insurance on individual homes has been greatly expanded. During the past eight years, the Federal Housing Administration alone insured over 2S million home mortgages valued at $27 billion, and in addition, insured more than ten million property improvement loans.

The Federal government must continue to provide leadership in order to make our cities and communities better places in which to live, work, and raise families, but without usurping rightful local authority, replacing individual responsibility, or stifling private initiative.

IMMIGRATION

Over 32,000 victims of Communist tyranny in Hungary were brought to our shores, and at this time our country is working to assist refugees from tyranny in Cuba.

Since 1953, the waiting period for naturalization applicants has been reduced from 18 months to 45 days.

The Administration also has made legislative recommendations to liberalize existing restrictions upon immigration while still safeguarding the national interest. It is imperative that our immigration policy be in the finest American tradition of providing a haven for oppressed peoples and fully in accord with our obligation as a leader of the free world.

VETERANS

In discharging the nation's obligation to our veterans, during the past eight years there have been:

The readjustment of World War II veterans was completed, and the five million Korean conflict veterans were assisted in achieving successful readjustment to civilian life;

Increases in compensation benefits for all eligible veterans with service connected disabilities;

Higher non-service connected pension benefits for needy veterans;

Greatly improved benefits to survivors of veterans dying in or as a result of service;

Authorization, by Presidential directive, of an increase in the number of beds available for sick and disabled veterans;

Development of a 12-year, $900 million construction program to modernize and improve our veterans hospitals;

New modern techniques brought into the administration of Veterans Affairs to provide the highest quality service possible to those who have defended us.

CONCLUSION

In concluding my final message to the Congress, it is fitting to look back to my first--to the aims and ideals I set forth on February 2, 1953: To use America's influence in world affairs to advance the cause of peace and justice, to conduct the affairs of the Executive Branch with integrity and efficiency, to encourage creative initiative in our economy, and to work toward the attainment of the well-being and equality of opportunity of all citizens.

Equally, we have honored our commitment to pursue and attain specific objectives. Among them, as stated eight years ago: strengthening of the mutual security program; development of world trade and commerce; ending of hostilities in Korea; creation of a powerful deterrent force; practicing fiscal responsibility; checking the menace of inflation; reducing the tax burden; providing an effective internal security program; developing and conserving our natural resources; reducing governmental interference in the affairs of the farmer; strengthening and improving services by the Department of Labor, and the vigilant guarding of civil and social fights.

I do not close this message implying that all is well--that all problems are solved. For progress implies both new and continuing problems and, unlike Presidential administrations, problems rarely have terminal dates.

Abroad, there is the continuing Communist threat to the freedom of Berlin, an explosive situation in Laos, the problems caused by Communist penetration of Cuba, as well as the many problems connected with the development of the new nations in Africa. These areas, in particular, call for delicate handling and constant review.

At home, several conspicuous problems remain: promoting higher levels of employment, with special emphasis on areas in which heavy unemployment has persisted; continuing to provide for steady economic growth and preserving a sound currency; bringing our balance of payments into more reasonable equilibrium and continuing a high level of confidence in our national and international systems; eliminating heavily excessive surpluses of a few farm commodities; and overcoming deficiencies in our health and educational programs.

Our goal always has been to add to the spiritual, moral, and material strength of our nation. I believe we have done this. But it is a process that must never end. Let us pray that leaders of both the near and distant future will be able to keep the nation strong and at peace, that they will advance the well-being of all our people, that they will lead us on to still higher moral standards, and that, in achieving these goals, they will maintain a reasonable balance between private and governmental responsibility.

Chapter 3

Additional Speeches

3.1   The Chance for Peace

In this spring of 1953 the free world weighs one question above all others: the chance for a just peace for all peoples.

To weigh this chance is to summon instantly to mind another recent moment of great decision. It came with that yet more hopeful spring of 1945, bright with the promise of victory and of freedom. The hope of all just men in that moment too was a just and lasting peace.

The eight years that have passed have seen that hope waver, grow dim, and almost die. And the shadow of fear again has darkly lengthened across the world.

Today the hope of free men remains stubborn and brave, but it is sternly disciplined by experience. It shuns not only all crude counsel of despair but also the self-deceit of easy illusion. It weighs the chance for peace with sure, clear knowledge of what happened to the vain hope of 1945.

In that spring of victory the soldiers of the Western Allies met the soldiers of Russia in the center of Europe. They were triumphant comrades in arms. Their peoples shared the joyous prospect of building, in honor of their dead, the only fitting monument-an age of just peace. All these war-weary peoples shared too this concrete, decent purpose: to guard vigilantly against the domination ever again of any part of the world by a single, unbridled aggressive power.

This common purpose lasted an instant and perished. The nations of the world divided to follow two distinct roads.

The United States and our valued friends, the other free nations, chose one road.

The leaders of the Soviet Union chose another.

The way chosen by the United States was plainly marked by a few clear precepts, which govern its conduct in world affairs.

1. No people on earth can be held, as a people, to be enemy, for all humanity shares the common hunger for peace and fellowship and justice.

2. No nation's security and well-being can be lastingly achieved in isolation but only in effective cooperation with fellow-nations.

3. Any nation's right to form of government and an economic system of its own choosing is inalienable.

4. Any nation's attempt to dictate to other nations their form of government is indefensible.

5. A nation's hope of lasting peace cannot be firmly based upon any race in armaments but rather upon just relations and honest understanding with all other nations.

In the light of these principles the citizens of the United States defined the way they proposed to follow, through the aftermath of war, toward true peace.

This way was faithful to the spirit that inspired the United Nations: to prohibit strife, to relieve tensions, to banish fears. This way was to control and to reduce armaments. This way was to allow all nations to devote their energies and resources to the great and good tasks of healing the war's wounds, of clothing and feeding and housing the needy, of perfecting a just political life, of enjoying the fruits of their own free toil.

The Soviet government held a vastly different vision of the future.

In the world of its design, security was to be found, not in mutual trust and mutual aid but in force: huge armies, subversion, rule of neighbor nations. The goal was power superiority at all costs. Security was to be sought by denying it to all others.

The result has been tragic for the world and, for the Soviet Union, it has also been ironic.

The amassing of the Soviet power alerted free nations to a new danger of aggression. It compelled them in self-defense to spend unprecedented money and energy for armaments. It forced them to develop weapons of war now capable of inflicting instant and terrible punishment upon any aggressor.

It instilled in the free nations, and let none doubt this, the unshakable conviction that, as long as there persists a threat to freedom, they must, at any cost, remain armed, strong, and ready for the risk of war.

It inspired them, and let none doubt this, to attain a unity of purpose and will beyond the power of propaganda or pressure to break, now or ever.

There remained, however, one thing essentially unchanged and unaffected by Soviet conduct: the readiness of the free nations to welcome sincerely any genuine evidence of peaceful purpose enabling all peoples again to resume their common quest of just peace.

The free nations, most solemnly and repeatedly, have assured the Soviet Union that their firm association has never had any aggressive purpose whatsoever. Soviet leaders, however, have seemed to persuade themselves, or tried to persuade their people, otherwise.

And so it has come to pass that the Soviet Union itself has shared and suffered the very fears it has fostered in the rest of the world.

This has been the way of life forged by eight years of fear and force.

What can the world, or any nation in it, hope for if no turning is found on this dread road?

The worst to be feared and the best to be expected can be simply stated.

The worst is atomic war.

The best would be this: a life of perpetual fear and tension; a burden of arms draining the wealth and the labor of all peoples; a wasting of strength that defies the American system or the Soviet system or any system to achieve true abundance and happiness for the peoples of this earth.

Every gun that is made, every warship launched, every rocket fired signifies, in the final sense, a theft from those who hunger and are not fed, those who are cold and are not clothed.

This world in arms is not spending money alone.

It is spending the sweat of its laborers, the genius of its scientists, the hopes of its children.

The cost of one modern heavy bomber is this: a modern brick school in more than 30 cities.

It is two electric power plants, each serving a town of 60,000 population.

It is two fine, fully equipped hospitals.

It is some 50 miles of concrete highway.

We pay for a single fighter with a half million bushels of wheat.

We pay for a single destroyer with new homes that could have housed more than 8,000 people.

This, I repeat, is the best way of life to be found on the road the world has been taking.

This is not a way of life at all, in any true sense. Under the cloud of threatening war, it is humanity hanging from a cross of iron.

These plain and cruel truths define the peril and point the hope that come with this spring of 1953.

This is one of those times in the affairs of nations when the gravest choices must be made, if there is to be a turning toward a just and lasting peace.

It is a moment that calls upon the governments of the world to speak their intentions with simplicity and with honesty.

It calls upon them to answer the questions that stirs the hearts of all sane men: is there no other way the world may live?

The world knows that an era ended with the death of Joseph Stalin. The extraordinary 30-year span of his rule saw the Soviet Empire expand to reach from the Baltic Sea to the Sea of Japan, finally to dominate 800 million souls.

The Soviet system shaped by Stalin and his predecessors was born of one World War. It survived the stubborn and often amazing courage of a second World War. It has lived to threaten a third.

Now, a new leadership has assumed power in the Soviet Union. It links to the past, however strong, cannot bind it completely. Its future is, in great part, its own to make.

This new leadership confronts a free world aroused, as rarely in its history, by the will to stay free.

This free world knows, out of bitter wisdom of experience, that vigilance and sacrifice are the price of liberty.

It knows that the defense of Western Europe imperatively demands the unity of purpose and action made possible by the North Atlantic Treaty Organization, embracing a European Defense Community.

It knows that Western Germany deserves to be a free and equal partner in this community and that this, for Germany, is the only safe way to full, final unity.

It knows that aggression in Korea and in southeast Asia are threats to the whole free community to be met by united action.

This is the kind of free world which the new Soviet leadership confront. It is a world that demands and expects the fullest respect of its rights and interests. It is a world that will always accord the same respect to all others.

So the new Soviet leadership now has a precious opportunity to awaken, with the rest of the world, to the point of peril reached and to help turn the tide of history.

Will it do this?

We do not yet know. Recent statements and gestures of Soviet leaders give some evidence that they may recognize this critical moment.

We welcome every honest act of peace.

We care nothing for mere rhetoric.

We are only for sincerity of peaceful purpose attested by deeds. The opportunities for such deeds are many. The performance of a great number of them waits upon no complex protocol but upon the simple will to do them. Even a few such clear and specific acts, such as the Soviet Union's signature upon the Austrian treaty or its release of thousands of prisoners still held from World War II, would be impressive signs of sincere intent. They would carry a power of persuasion not to be matched by any amount of oratory.

This we do know: a world that begins to witness the rebirth of trust among nations can find its way to a peace that is neither partial nor punitive.

With all who will work in good faith toward such a peace, we are ready, with renewed resolve, to strive to redeem the near-lost hopes of our day.

The first great step along this way must be the conclusion of an honorable armistice in Korea.

This means the immediate cessation of hostilities and the prompt initiation of political discussions leading to the holding of free elections in a united Korea.

It should mean, no less importantly, an end to the direct and indirect attacks upon the security of Indochina and Malaya. For any armistice in Korea that merely released aggressive armies to attack elsewhere would be fraud.

We seek, throughout Asia as throughout the world, a peace that is true and total.

Out of this can grow a still wider task-the achieving of just political settlements for the other serious and specific issues between the free world and the Soviet Union.

None of these issues, great or small, is insoluble-given only the will to respect the rights of all nations.

Again we say: the United States is ready to assume its just part.

We have already done all within our power to speed conclusion of the treaty with Austria, which will free that country from economic exploitation and from occupation by foreign troops.

We are ready not only to press forward with the present plans for closer unity of the nations of Western Europe but also, upon that foundation, to strive to foster a broader European community, conducive to the free movement of persons, of trade, and of ideas.

This community would include a free and united Germany, with a government based upon free and secret elections.

This free community and the full independence of the East European nations could mean the end of the present unnatural division of Europe.

As progress in all these areas strengthens world trust, we could proceed concurrently with the next great work-the reduction of the burden of armaments now weighing upon the world. To this end we would welcome and enter into the most solemn agreements. These could properly include:

The limitation, by absolute numbers or by an agreed international ratio, of the sizes of the military and security forces of all nations. A commitment by all nations to set an agreed limit upon that proportion of total production of certain strategic materials to be devoted to military purposes.

International control of atomic energy to promote its use for peaceful purposes only and to insure the prohibition of atomic weapons. A limitation or prohibition of other categories of weapons of great destructiveness.

The enforcement of all these agreed limitations and prohibitions by adequate safe-guards, including a practical system of inspection under the United Nations. The details of such disarmament programs are manifestly critical and complex. Neither the United States nor any other nation can properly claim to possess a perfect, immutable formula. But the formula matters less than the faith-the good faith without which no formula can work justly and effectively.

The fruit of success in all these tasks would present the world with the greatest task, and the greatest opportunity, of all. It is this: the dedication of the energies, the resources, and the imaginations of all peaceful nations to a new kind of war. This would be a declared total war, not upon any human enemy but upon the brute forces of poverty and need.

The peace we seek, founded upon decent trust and cooperative effort among nations, can be fortified, not by weapons of war but by wheat and by cotton, by milk and by wool, by meat and by timber and by rice. These are words that translate into every language on earth. These are needs that challenge this world in arms.

This idea of a just and peaceful world is not new or strange to us. It inspired the people of the United States to initiate the European Recovery Program in 1947. That program was prepared to treat, with like and equal concern, the needs of Eastern and Western Europe.

We are prepared to reaffirm, with the most concrete evidence, our readiness to help build a world in which all peoples can be productive and prosperous.

This Government is ready to ask its people to join with all nations in devoting a substantial percentage of the savings achieved by disarmament to a fund for world aid and reconstruction. The purposes of this great work would be to help other peoples to develop the underdeveloped areas of the world, to stimulate profitability and fair world trade, to assist all peoples to know the blessings of productive freedom.

The monuments to this new kind of war would be these: roads and schools, hospitals and homes, food and health.

We are ready, in short, to dedicate our strength to serving the needs, rather than the fears, of the world.

We are ready, by these and all such actions, to make of the United Nations an institution that can effectively guard the peace and security of all peoples.

I know of nothing I can add to make plainer the sincere purpose of the United States.

I know of no course, other than that marked by these and similar actions, that can be called the highway of peace.

I know of only one question upon which progress waits. It is this:

What is the Soviet Union ready to do?

Whatever the answer be, let it be plainly spoken.

Again we say: the hunger for peace is too great, the hour in history too late, for any government to mock men's hopes with mere words and promises and gestures.

The test of truth is simple. There can be no persuasion but by deeds.

Is the new leadership of the Soviet Union prepared to use its decisive influence in the Communist world, including control of the flow of arms, to bring not merely an expedient truce in Korea but genuine peace in Asia?

Is it prepared to allow other nations, including those of Eastern Europe, the free choice of their own forms of government?

Is it prepared to act in concert with others upon serious disarmament proposals to be made firmly effective by stringent U.N. control and inspection?

If not, where then is the concrete evidence of the Soviet Union's concern for peace?

The test is clear.

There is, before all peoples, a precious chance to turn the black tide of events. If we failed to strive to seize this chance, the judgment of future ages would be harsh and just.

If we strive but fail and the world remains armed against itself, it at least need be divided no longer in its clear knowledge of who has condemned humankind to this fate.

The purpose of the United States, in stating these proposals, is simple and clear.

These proposals spring, without ulterior purpose or political passion, from our calm conviction that the hunger for peace is in the hearts of all peoples--those of Russia and of China no less than of our own country.

They conform to our firm faith that God created men to enjoy, not destroy, the fruits of the earth and of their own toil.

They aspire to this: the lifting, from the backs and from the hearts of men, of their burden of arms and of fears, so that they may find before them a golden age of freedom and of peace.

3.2   Atoms for Peace Speech, President Eisenhower, December 8, 1953

Madame President, Members of the General Assembly:

When Secretary General Hammarskjöld's invitation to address this General Assembly reached me in Bermuda, I was just beginning a series of conferences with the Prime Ministers and Foreign Ministers of Great Britain and of France. Our subject was some of the problems that beset our world.

During the remainder of the Bermuda Conference, I had constantly in mind that ahead of me lay a great honor. That honor is mine today as I stand here, Privileged to address the General Assembly of the United Nations.

At the same time that I appreciate the distinction of addressing you, I have a sense of exhilaration as I look upon this Assembly.

Never before in history has so much hope for so many people been gathered together in a single organization. Your deliberations and decisions during these somber years have already realized part of those hopes.

But the great test and the great accomplishments still lie ahead. And in the confident expectation of those accomplishments, I would use the office which, for the time being, I hold, to assure you that the Government of the United States will remain steadfast in its support of this body. This we shall do in the conviction that you will provide a great share of the wisdom, the courage, and the faith which can bring to this world lasting peace for all nations, and happiness and well-being for all men.

Clearly, it would not be fitting for me to take this occasion to present to you a unilateral American report on Bermuda. Nevertheless, I assure you that in our deliberations on that lovely island we sought to invoke those same great concepts of universal peace and human dignity which are so clearly etched in your Charter.

Neither would it be a measure of this great opportunity merely to recite, however hopefully, pious platitudes.

I therefore decided that this occasion warranted my saying to you some of the things that have been on the minds and hearts of my legislative and executive associates and on mine for a great many months-thoughts I had originally planned to say primarily to the American people.

I know that the American people share my deep belief that if a danger exists in the world, it is a danger shared by all--and equally, that if hope exists in the mind of one nation, that hope should be shared by all.

Finally, if there is to be advanced any proposal designed to ease even by the smallest measure the tensions of today's world, what more appropriate audience could there be than the members of the General Assembly of the United Nations?

I feel impelled to speak today in a language that in a sense is new--one which I, who has spent so much of my life in the military profession, would have preferred never to use.

That new language is the language of atomic warfare.

The atomic age has moved forward at such a pace that every citizen of the world should have some comprehension, at least in comparative terms, of the extent of this development of the utmost significance to every one of us. Clearly, if the people of the world are to conduct an intelligent search for peace, they must be armed with the significant facts of today's existence.

My recital of atomic danger and power is necessarily stated in United States terms, for these are the only in controvertible facts that I know. I need hardly point out to this Assembly, however, that this subject is global, not merely national in character.

On July 16, 1945, the United States set off the world's first atomic explosion. Since that date in 1945, the United States of America has conducted 42 test explosions.

Atomic bombs today are more than 25 times as powerful as the weapons with which the atomic age dawned, while hydrogen weapons are in the ranges of millions of tons of TNT equivalent.

Today, the United States' stockpile of atomic weapons, which, of course, increases daily, exceeds by many times the explosive equivalent of the total of all bombs and all shells that came from every plane and every gun in every theatre of war in all of the years of World War II.

A single air group, whether afloat or land-based, can now deliver to any reachable target a destructive cargo exceeding in power all the bombs that fell on Britain in all of World War II.

In size and variety, the development of atomic weapons has been no less remarkable. The development has been such that atomic weapons have virtually achieved conventional status within our armed services. In the United States, the Army, the Navy, the Air Force, and the Marine Corps are all capable of putting this weapon to military use.

But the dread secret, and the fearful engines of atomic might, are not ours alone.

In the first place, the secret is possessed by our friends and allies, Great Britain and Canada, whose scientific genius made a tremendous contribution to our original discoveries, and the designs of atomic bombs.

The secret is also known by the Soviet Union.

The Soviet Union has informed us that, over recent years, it has devoted extensive resources to atomic weapons. During this period, the Soviet Union has exploded a series of atomic devices, including at least one involving thermo-nuclear reactions.

If at one time the United States possessed what might have been called a monopoly of atomic power, that monopoly ceased to exist several years ago. Therefore, although our earlier start has permitted us to accumulate what is today a great quantitative advantage, the atomic realities of today comprehend two facts of even greater significance.

First, the knowledge now possessed by several nations will eventually be shared by others--possibly all others.

Second, even a vast superiority in numbers of weapons, and a consequent capability of devastating retaliation, is no preventive, of itself, against the fearful material damage and toll of human lives that would be inflicted by surprise aggression.

The free world, at least dimly aware of these facts, has naturally embarked on a large program of warning and defense systems. That program will be accelerated and expanded.

But let no one think that the expenditure of vast sums for weapons and systems of defense can guarantee absolute safety for the cities and citizens of any nation. The awful arithmetic of the atomic bomb does not permit any such easy solution. Even against the most powerful defense, an aggressor in possession of the effective minimum number of atomic bombs for a surprise attack could probably place a sufficient number of his bombs on the chosen targets to cause hideous damage.

Should such an atomic attack be launched against the United States, our reactions would be swift and resolute. But for me to say that the defense capabilities of the United States are such that they could inflict terrible losses upon an aggressor-- for me to say that the retaliation capabilities of the United States are so great that such an aggressor's land would be laid waste--all this, while fact, is not the true expression of the purpose and the hope of the United States.

To pause there would be to confirm the hopeless finality of a belief that two atomic colossi are doomed malevolently to eye each other indefinitely across a trembling world. To stop there would be to accept helplessly the probability of civilization destroyed--the annihilation of the irreplaceable heritage of mankind handed down to us generation from generation--and the condemnation of mankind to begin all over again the age-old struggle upward from savagery toward decency, and right, and justice.

Surely no sane member of the human race could discover victory in such desolation. Could anyone wish his name to be coupled by history with such human degradation and destruction.

Occasional pages of history do record the faces of the "Great Destroyers" but the whole book of history reveals mankind's never-ending quest for peace, and mankind's God-given capacity to build.

It is with the book of history, and not with isolated pages, that the United States will ever wish to be identified. My country wants to be constructive, not destructive. It wants agreement, not wars, among nations. It wants itself to live in freedom, and in the confidence that the people of every other nation enjoy equally the right of choosing their own way of life.

So my country's purpose is to help us move out of the dark chamber of horrors into the light, to find a way by which the minds of men, the hopes of men, the souls of men every where, can move forward toward peace and happiness and well being.

In this quest, I know that we must not lack patience.

I know that in a world divided, such as our today, salvation cannot be attained by one dramatic act.

I know that many steps will have to be taken over many months before the world can look at itself one day and truly realize that a new climate of mutually peaceful confidence is abroad in the world.

But I know, above all else, that we much start to take these steps--now.

The United States and its allies, Great Britain and France, have over the past months tried to take some of these steps. Let no one say that we shun the conference table.

On the record has long stood the request of the United States, Great Britain, and France to negotiate with the Soviet Union the problems of a divided Germany.

On that record has long stood the request of the same three nations to negotiate the problems of Korea.

Most recently, we have received from the Soviet Union what is in effect an expression of willingness to hold a Four Power meeting. Along with our allies, Great Britain and France, we were pleased to see that this note did not contain the unacceptable preconditions previously put forward.

As you already know from our joint Bermuda communiqué, the United States, Great Britain, and France have agreed promptly to meet with the Soviet Union.

The Government of the United States approaches this conference with hopeful sincerity. We will bend every effort of our minds to the single purpose of emerging from that conference with tangible results toward peace--the only true way of lessening international tension.

We never have, we never will, propose or suggest that the Soviet Union surrender what is rightfully theirs.

We will never say that the people of Russia are an enemy with whom we have no desire ever to deal or mingle in friendly and fruitful relationship.

On the contrary, we hope that this coming Conference may initiate a relationship with the Soviet Union which will eventually bring about a free inter mingling of the peoples of the east and of the west--the one sure, human way of developing the understanding required for confident and peaceful relations.

Instead of the discontent which is now settling upon Eastern Germany, occupied Austria, and countries of Eastern Europe, we seek a harmonious family of free European nations, with none a threat to the other, and least of all a threat to the peoples of Russia.

Beyond the turmoil and strife and misery of Asia, we seek peaceful opportunity for these peoples to develop their natural resources and to elevate their lives.

These are not idle works or shallow visions. Behind them lies a story of nations lately come to independence, not as a result of war, but through free grant or peaceful negotiation. There is a record, already written, of assistance gladly given by nations of the west to needy peoples, and to those suffering the temporary effects of famine, drought, and natural disaster.

These are deeds of peace. They speak more loudly than promises or protestations of peaceful intent.

But I do not wish to rest either upon the reiteration of past proposals or the restatement of past deeds. The gravity of the time is such that every new avenue of peace, no matter how dimly discernible, should be explored.

These is at least one new avenue of peace which has not yet been well explored--an avenue now laid out by the General Assembly of the United Nations.

In its resolution of November 18th, 1953 this General Assembly suggested--and I quote--"that the Disarmament Commission study the desirability of establishing a sub-committee consisting of representatives of the Powers principally involved, which should seek in private an acceptable solution . . . and report on such a solution to the General Assembly and to the Security Council not later than 1 September 1954."

The United States, heeding the suggestion of the General Assembly of the United Nations, is instantly prepared to meet privately with such other countries as may be "principally involved," to seek "an acceptable solution" to the atomic armaments race which over shadows not only the peace, but the very life, of the world.

We shall carry into these private or diplomatic talks a new conception.

The United States would seek more than the mere reduction or elimination of atomic materials for military purposes.

It is not enough to take this weapon out of the hands of the soldiers. It must be put into the hands of those who will know how to strip its military casing and adapt it to the arts of peace.

The United States knows that if the fearful trend of atomic military build up can be reversed, this greatest of destructive forces can be developed into a great boon, for the benefit of all mankind.

The United States knows that peaceful power from atomic energy is no dream of the future. That capability, already proved, is here--now--today. Who can doubt, if the entire body of the world's scientists and engineers had adequate amounts of fissionable material with which to test and develop their ideas, that this capability would rapidly be transformed into universal, efficient, and economic usage.

To hasten the day when fear of the atom will begin to disappear from the minds of people, and the governments of the East and West, there are certain steps that can be taken now.

I therefore make the following proposals:

The Governments principally involved, to the extent permitted by elementary prudence, to begin now and continue to make joint contributions from their stockpiles of normal uranium and fissionable materials to an international Atomic

Energy Agency. We would expect that such an agency would be set up under the aegis of the United Nations.

The ratios of contributions, the procedures and other details would properly be within the scope of the "private conversations" I have referred to earlier.

The United States is prepared to under take these explorations in good faith. Any partner of the United States acting in the same good faith will find the United States a not unreasonable or ungenerous associate.

Undoubtedly initial and early contributions to this plan would be small in quantity. However, the proposal has the great virtue that it can be under taken without the irritations and mutual suspicions incident to any attempt to set up a completely acceptable system of world-wide inspection and control.

The Atomic Energy Agency could be made responsible for the impounding, storage, and protection of the contributed fissionable and other materials. The ingenuity of our scientists will provide special safe conditions under which such a bank of fissionable material can be made essentially immune to surprise seizure.

The more important responsibility of this Atomic Energy Agency would be to devise methods where by this fissionable material would be allocated to serve the peaceful pursuits of mankind. Experts would be mobilized to apply atomic energy to the needs of agriculture, medicine, and other peaceful activities. A special purpose would be to provide abundant electrical energy in the power-starved areas of the world. Thus the contributing powers would be dedicating some of their strength to serve the needs rather than the fears of mankind.

The United States would be more than willing--it would be proud to take up with others "principally involved: the development of plans where by such peaceful use of atomic energy would be expedited.

Of those "principally involved" the Soviet Union must, of course, be one.

I would be prepared to submit to the Congress of the United States, and with every expectation of approval, any such plan that would:

First--encourage world-wide investigation into the most effective peace time uses of fissionable material, and with the certainty that they had all the material needed for the conduct of all experiments that were appropriate;

Second--begin to diminish the potential destructive power of the world's atomic stockpiles;

Third--allow all peoples of all nations to see that, in this enlightened age, the great powers of the earth, both of the East and of the West, are interested in human aspirations first, rather than in building up the armaments of war;

Fourth--open up a new channel for peaceful discussion, and initiate at least a new approach to the many difficult problems that must be solved in both private and public conversations, if the world is to shake off the inertia imposed by fear, and is to make positive progress toward peace.

Against the dark background of the atomic bomb, the United Stats does not wish merely to present strength, but also the desire and the hope for peace.

The coming months will be fraught with fateful decisions. In this Assembly; in the capitals and military headquarters of the world; in the hearts of men every where, be they governors, or governed, may they be decisions which will lead this work out of fear and into peace.

To the making of these fateful decisions, the United States pledges before you--and therefore before the world--its determination to help solve the fearful atomic dilemma--to devote its entire heart and mind to find the way by which the miraculous inventiveness of man shall not be dedicated to his death, but consecrated to his life.

I again thank the delegates for the great honor they have done me, in inviting me to appear before them, and in listening to me so courteously. Thank you.

3.3 Eisenhower's farewell address

Versions of *Eisenhower's farewell address* include:

- Eisenhower's farewell address (audio transcript)
- Eisenhower's farewell address (reading copy)
- Eisenhower's farewell address (press copy)

Chapter 4

Text and image sources, contributors, and licenses

4.1 Text

- **Dwight Eisenhower's First Inaugural Address** *Source:* https://en.wikisource.org/wiki/Dwight_Eisenhower'{}s_First_Inaugural_Address?oldid=4475289 *Contributors:* Zhaladshar, Danny~enwikisource, Politicaljunkie, Pathosbot, Billinghurst, SDrewthbot, CandalBot and Anonymous: 5

- **Dwight Eisenhower's Second Inaugural Address** *Source:* https://en.wikisource.org/wiki/Dwight_Eisenhower'{}s_Second_Inaugural_Address?oldid=2848667 *Contributors:* Danny~enwikisource, Politicaljunkie, Pathosbot, Billinghurst, SDrewthbot, Nantucketnoon and Anonymous: 5

- **Dwight D. Eisenhower's First State of the Union Address** *Source:* https://en.wikisource.org/wiki/Dwight_D._Eisenhower'{}s_First_State_of_the_Union_Address?oldid=4791427 *Contributors:* Zhaladshar, Danny~enwikisource, Politicaljunkie, Pathosbot, ZSBot, AdamBMorgan, SDrewthbot, Spydyspydy and Anonymous: 2

- **Dwight D. Eisenhower's Second State of the Union Address** *Source:* https://en.wikisource.org/wiki/Dwight_D._Eisenhower'{}s_Second_State_of_the_Union_Address?oldid=4791423 *Contributors:* Zhaladshar, Danny~enwikisource, Politicaljunkie, Pathosbot, ZSBot, AdamB-Morgan, SDrewthbot, Spydyspydy and Anonymous: 4

- **Dwight D. Eisenhower's Third State of the Union Address** *Source:* https://en.wikisource.org/wiki/Dwight_D._Eisenhower'{}s_Third_State_of_the_Union_Address?oldid=4790927 *Contributors:* Danny~enwikisource, Politicaljunkie, Pathosbot, ZSBot, SDrewthbot, Spydyspydy and Anonymous: 2

- **Dwight D. Eisenhower's Fourth State of the Union Address** *Source:* https://en.wikisource.org/wiki/Dwight_D._Eisenhower'{}s_Fourth_State_of_the_Union_Address?oldid=4790930 *Contributors:* Danny~enwikisource, Politicaljunkie, Pathosbot, ZSBot, SDrewthbot, Spydyspydy and Anonymous: 2

- **Dwight D. Eisenhower's Fifth State of the Union Address** *Source:* https://en.wikisource.org/wiki/Dwight_D._Eisenhower'{}s_Fifth_State_of_the_Union_Address?oldid=4790938 *Contributors:* Danny~enwikisource, Politicaljunkie, Pathosbot, ZSBot, SDrewthbot, Spydyspydy and Anonymous: 3

- **Dwight D. Eisenhower's Sixth State of the Union Address** *Source:* https://en.wikisource.org/wiki/Dwight_D._Eisenhower'{}s_Sixth_State_of_the_Union_Address?oldid=4790935 *Contributors:* Danny~enwikisource, Politicaljunkie, Pathosbot, ZSBot, SDrewthbot, Spydyspydy and Anonymous: 2

- **Dwight D. Eisenhower's Seventh State of the Union Address** *Source:* https://en.wikisource.org/wiki/Dwight_D._Eisenhower'{}s_Seventh_State_of_the_Union_Address?oldid=4790940 *Contributors:* Danny~enwikisource, Politicaljunkie, Pathosbot, ZSBot, Dromioofephesus, SDrewthbot, Spydyspydy and Anonymous: 1

- **Dwight D. Eisenhower's Eighth State of the Union Address** *Source:* https://en.wikisource.org/wiki/Dwight_D._Eisenhower'{}s_Eighth_State_of_the_Union_Address?oldid=4790942 *Contributors:* Danny~enwikisource, Politicaljunkie, Pathosbot, ZSBot, Dromioofephesus, SDrewthbot, Spydyspydy and Anonymous: 1

- **Dwight D. Eisenhower's Ninth State of the Union Address** *Source:* https://en.wikisource.org/wiki/Dwight_D._Eisenhower'{}s_Ninth_State_of_the_Union_Address?oldid=4790943 *Contributors:* Danny~enwikisource, Politicaljunkie, Pathosbot, ZSBot, Dromioofephesus, SDrewthbot, Spydyspydy and Anonymous: 2

- **The Chance for Peace** *Source:* https://en.wikisource.org/wiki/The_Chance_for_Peace?oldid=5566418 *Contributors:* Pharos, Sherurcij, Pathosbot, MrDolomite, ZSBot, SebastianHelm, Dromioofephesus, SDrewthbot, Mattisse, Simon Peter Hughes and Anonymous: 2

- **Atoms for Peace Speech, President Eisenhower, December 8, 1953** *Source:* https://en.wikisource.org/wiki/Atoms_for_Peace_Speech%2C_President_Eisenhower%2C_December_8%2C_1953?oldid=6310389 *Contributors:* Billinghurst, SDrewthbot, NPguy and שילוני

- **Eisenhower's farewell address** *Source:* https://en.wikisource.org/wiki/Eisenhower'{}s_farewell_address?oldid=3850587 *Contributors:* Prosody

4.2   Images

- **File:PD-icon.svg** *Source:* https://upload.wikimedia.org/wikipedia/commons/6/62/PD-icon.svg *License:* Public domain *Contributors:* Created by uploader. Based on similar symbols. *Original artist:* Various. See log. (Original SVG was based on File:PD-icon.png by Duesentrieb, which was based on Image:Red copyright.png by Rfl.)
- **File:US-GreatSeal-Obverse.svg** *Source:* https://upload.wikimedia.org/wikipedia/commons/5/5c/Great_Seal_of_the_United_States_%28obverse% 29.svg *License:* Public domain *Contributors:* Extracted from PDF version of *Our Flag*, available here (direct PDF URL here.) *Original artist:* U.S. Government

4.3   Content license

- Creative Commons Attribution-Share Alike 3.0

www.ingramcontent.com/pod-product-compliance
Lightning Source LLC
Chambersburg PA
CBHW081841280526
45789CB00007B/2534